OUR WAY
AND OUR LIFE

Christ in His Mysteries

⊕

OUR WAY
AND OUR LIFE

Christ in His Mysteries

☩

Blessed Columba Marmion

Angelico Press

Angelico Press reprint edition, 2013
This Angelico edition is a republication of the
work originally published as *Our Way and Our Life*
(an abridged edition of *Christ in His Mysteries*)
by Sands & Co., London, 1927

No part of this book may be reproduced or transmitted,
in any form or by any means, without permission

For information, address:
Angelico Press, 4619 Slayden Rd., NE
Tacoma, WA 98422
www.angelicopress.com

ISBN: 978-1-887593-03-8
ISBN: 978-1-62138-629-2

Cover Design: Cristy Deming

Image Credit: James Tissot (French, 1836–1902)
Jesus Appears to the Holy Women
Brooklyn Museum, Purchased by
public subscription, 00.159.337

CONTENTS

Translator's Foreword

IT has been suggested that a condensed edition of *Christ in His Mysteries* would be welcomed by those who have not opportunity and leisure to read the larger volume where the subjects of the conferences are developed at greater length.

With permission of the Editor of the late Abbot Columba Marmion's works, the translator has been happy to undertake this task.

A Nun of Tyburn Convent

Feast of Christ the King, 1926

I

Our Contact with
the Mysteries of Jesus

THE MYSTERIES that Jesus, the Word Incarnate, lived here below were lived for us. In them He shows Himself as our model, but above all, He wills to make Himself one with our souls as being the Head of one Mystical Body whereof we are the members.

Such is the power of these mysteries that it is always active and effectual. From Heaven, where He is seated at the right hand of God His Father, Christ continues to communicate the fruit of the different phases of His life to our souls so as to realize in them a divine resemblance to Himself.

Participation in the mysteries of Jesus requires the co-operation of the soul. If God reveals the secrets of His love towards us it is in order that we may accept them, that we may enter into His views and designs, and adapt ourselves to the Eternal Plan apart from which neither holiness nor salvation is possible. If Christ opens to us the unfathomable treasures of His states and mysteries it is that we may draw upon them and make them our own.

But we do not seek for that which we know not. The will does not attach itself to a good that the intellect does not set before it: *Ignoti nulla cupido.*

Now that Christ has taken His sensible presence from us how are we to know His mysteries, their beauty, harmony, virtue, and power? Above all, what are we to do in order to be put into life-giving contact with them?

The knowledge of Jesus and of the various stages of His life is to be gained first of all from the Gospels.

It is enough for us to read these sacred pages so simple and so sublime—that is to say if we read them with faith—in order to see and hear Christ Himself. For this Book is inspired. Light and power go out from it to enlighten and strengthen souls that are upright and sincere. Happy are they who open it every day! They drink at the very well-spring of living waters.

Another way of coming to the knowledge of Jesus and of His mysteries is by associating ourselves with the Church in her Liturgy.

Before ascending into Heaven, Christ said to the Apostles upon whom He founded His Church: "All power is given to Me in Heaven and in earth. . . . As the Father hath sent Me, I also send you. . . . He that heareth you, heareth Me. . . ." This is why the Church is like an extension, throughout the ages, of the Incarnation; she replaces Jesus with us; she has inherited the divine tenderness of her Heavenly Bridegroom; from Him she has received as dowry, with the power of sanctifying souls, the riches of grace acquired by Jesus upon the Cross on the day of their mystical espousals.

All proportion guarded, we can then say of the Church what her Bridegroom said of Himself; she is for us the way, the truth, and the life. She is the way because we only come to God through Christ Jesus, and we can only be united to Christ by being incorporated (in fact or in desire) in the Church through baptism. She is the truth, because, with all the authority of her Founder, she has the custody of the truth brought to us by Revelation which she proposes to our acceptance and belief. Finally, she is the life because by the public worship which she alone has the right of organizing, by the sacraments which she alone administers, she distributes the life of grace to souls and maintains it within them.

We know that it is especially by the Liturgy that the Church brings up the souls of her children that she may perfect in them that image of Christ which is the very form of our predestination.

Guided by the Holy Spirit, the Spirit of Jesus Himself, the Church each year unfolds before the eyes of her children the complete cycle of Christ's mysteries, sometimes greatly abridged, sometimes in their exact chronological order as during Holy Week and Paschal time. She thus causes each mystery of her Divine Bridegroom to be vividly represented and lived over again; she makes us pass through each stage of His life. If we allow ourselves to be guided by her, we shall infallibly come to know the mysteries of Jesus, and above all we shall enter into the thoughts and feelings of His Divine Heart.

The Church, knowing well the secret of her Bridegroom, takes from the Gospel the pages which best place each of these mysteries in relief; then, with perfect art, she illustrates them with passages of the psalms, prophecies, the epistles of St. Paul and the other Apostles, and with selections from the Fathers of the Church. She thus places the teachings of the Divine Master, the details of His life and the substance of His mysteries in a clearer and fuller light.

At the same time, by the choice of readings from the Holy Scriptures and sacred authors, by the aspirations that she suggests to us, by her symbolism and ritual, she places our souls in the attitude demanded by these mysteries, she fosters in our hearts the requisite dispositions for assimilating the spiritual fruit of each mystery in the greatest possible measure.

For although it is ever the same Jesus pursuing the same work of our sanctification, each mystery is a fresh manifestation of Christ for us; each has its special beauty, its particular splendour, as likewise its own grace. The grace that flows for us from the Feast of the Nativity has not the same character as that which the celebration of the Passion brings to us. We ought to rejoice at Christmas, just as we ought to feel sorrow for our sins when we contemplate the unutterable sufferings whereby Christ expiated them. In the same way the inward joy that floods our souls at

Easter arises from another source and has another splendour than that which thrills us when we celebrate the coming of our Saviour upon earth.

The Fathers of the Church speak more than once of what they call the *vis mysterii*, the virtue and signification of the mystery which is being celebrated. In each of Christ's mysteries we may apply to Christians what St. Gregory of Nazianzen said to the faithful at the Feast of Easter: "We cannot offer a gift more pleasing to God than to offer ourselves with a perfect understanding of the mystery." *Nihil autem daturus est tantum, quantum si se ipse obtulerit hujus mysterii rationem probe intelligentem.*

Some there are who see nothing in the celebration of Christ's mysteries beyond the perfection of the ceremonies, the harmony of the ritual, etc. And all these things are excellent as far as they go.

First of all because the Church, Christ's Bride, having herself regulated all the details of the worship of her Bridegroom, their perfect observance honours God and His Son Jesus. Bossuet says: "It is an established law for all the mysteries of Christianity, that to reach our intelligence they must first be placed before our senses. This had to be so in order to honour Him Who, being invisible by nature, willed to appear under a visible form for love of us."

It is besides a psychological law of our nature—matter and spirit—that we should pass from the visible to the invisible. The outward elements of the celebration of the mysteries serve as rungs in a ladder whereby our souls may rise to the contemplation and love of heavenly and supernatural realities. This is, as we sing at Christmas, the dispensation of the Incarnation itself: *Ut dum visibiliter Deum cognoscimus,* PER HUNC *in invisibilium amorem* RAPIAMUR.

These outward elements, therefore, have their use, but we must not exclusively stop at them; they are but the fringe of Christ's garment; the virtue of His mysteries is before all interior, and it is this virtue that we must especially seek. Holy Church asks of God in the post-communion of several feasts to give us the right apprehension of the virtue proper to the mystery being celebrated, so that we may be penetrated by it and live thereby. This is to know Christ "in all wisdom and spiritual understanding."

When Jesus was upon earth "virtue went out from Him, and healed all": *Virtus de illo exibat et sanabat omnes.* Christ Jesus is ever the same; if with faith we contemplate His mysteries, either in the Gospel or in the Liturgy that the Church sets before us, the grace that He merited for us when He lived these mysteries is produced within us.

The mysteries of Jesus are states of His Sacred Humanity. All His graces came from His Divinity in order to be communicated to His Humanity, and, through His Humanity, to each member of His Mystical Body: *Secundum mensuram donationis Christi.* In taking a human nature from our race, the Word, so to speak, espoused all humanity to Himself, and—in a measure known to God, and proportioned, in what regards ourselves, to the degree of our faith—every soul shares in the grace that inundates Christ's blessed soul.

Each of Christ's mysteries, representing a state of His Sacred Humanity, thus brings to us a special participation in His Divinity. For example, at Christmas we celebrate Christ's Birth at Bethlehem. He takes a human nature from us in order to make us partakers of His Divine nature, and each Christmas, worthily celebrated, is, by a more abundant communication of grace for the soul, like a new birth to divine life. Upon Calvary we die to sin with Christ; Jesus gives us the grace to detest more deeply all that offends Him. During Paschaltide we share in that liberty of soul, in that more intense life for God of which He is the Model in His Resurrection. On the day of His Ascension we ascend with Him to Heaven, to be, by faith and desire, with the Heavenly Father in the intimacy of the sanctuary of the Divinity.

Following Christ Jesus in this manner throughout all His mysteries, uniting ourselves to Him, we share, little by little but surely, and each time more fully and deeply, in His Divinity and His Divine life.

The Sovereign Pontiff Pius X wrote in his encyclical of November 23rd, 1903, that "the active participation of the faithful in the sacred mysteries and in the public and solemn prayers of the Church is *the first and indispensable source of the Christian spirit.*"

On this subject there is indeed a truth of great importance which is too often forgotten and even sometimes unknown.

Man can imitate Christ in two ways. We can strive to imitate Him by merely natural efforts, as when we aim at reproducing a human ideal presented by some hero or other personage whom we love or admire. There are people who think that it is in this manner we must imitate Our Lord and reproduce in ourselves the traits of His Adorable Person.

This is to lose sight of the truth that Christ is a Divine Model. His human beauty and virtues have their roots in His Divinity and thence derive all their splendour. We can and certainly must with the help of grace make every effort to comprehend Christ and to model our virtues and actions upon His, but the Holy Spirit—*Digitus paternæ dexteræ*—is alone capable of reproducing within us the true image of the Son, because our imitation must be of a supernatural order.

Now this work of the Divine Artist is especially wrought in prayer based upon faith and enkindled by love. While, with the eyes of faith and with the love that yearns to give itself, we contemplate Christ's mysteries, the Holy Spirit, Who is the Spirit of Christ, acts within our inmost soul and fashions it in such a way by His sovereignly effectual touches as to reproduce within it, as by a sacramental virtue, the traits of the Divine Model.

This is why the contemplation of the mysteries of Jesus is so fruitful in itself; this is why the essentially supernatural contact with the different phases of the life of her Bridegroom, into which the Church places us by means of the Liturgy, is so vital for us.

There is no surer way, no more infallible means, of making us one with Christ.

II

Advent

Divine Preparations

G OD'S eternal design of sending His own Son into the world to redeem the human race, lost and disgraced by sin, and of restoring to it the children's rights of heavenly inheritance and beatitude, is the masterpiece of His wisdom and love. God's ways of seeing things are not our ways. All His thoughts are higher than ours as the heavens are higher than the earth, but it is especially in the work of the Incarnation and Redemption that the sublimity and greatness of the Divine ways shine forth. This work, so closely united to the very life of the Blessed Trinity, remained throughout long ages hidden in the depths of the Divine secrets: *Sacramentum absconditum a sæculis in Deo.*

Why did God choose to delay the coming of His Son amongst us for so many centuries? We cannot, mere creatures as we are, fathom the depths of the reasons why God accomplishes His works under such or such conditions. He is the infinitely Supreme Being Who has no need of a counsellor. But as He is likewise Wisdom that reacheth "from end to end mightily, and ordereth all things sweetly," we may yet humbly seek to learn something of the appropriateness of the conditions of His mysteries.

It was fitting that men having sinned by pride should be obliged, by the prolonged experience of their weakness and the extent of their misery, to confess their absolute need of a Redeemer and to yearn for His coming with all the fibres of their nature.

The thought of this future Redeemer is apparent throughout the Old Testament wherein all symbols, rites, and sacrifices prefigure Him. All desires converge towards Him. The religion of Israel was the expectation of the Messias.

Moreover, the greatness of the mystery of the Incarnation and the majesty of the Redeemer demanded that the revelation of Him to the human race should only be made by degrees. Man, on the morrow of his fall, was neither worthy of receiving nor capable of welcoming the full manifestation of the God-Man. It was by a dispensation at once full of wisdom and mercy that God disclosed this ineffable mystery only little by little, by the mouth of the Prophets. When the human race should be sufficiently prepared, the Word, so many times announced, so often promised, would Himself appear here below to instruct us: *Multifariam multisque modis olim Deus loquens patribus in prophetis . . . novissime locutus est nobis in Filio.*

As we know, it was just after the sin of our first parents, in the very cradle of the already rebellious human race, that God began to reveal the mystery of the Incarnation.

Adam and Eve prostrate before their Creator, in the shame and despair of their fall, dare not raise their eyes to heaven. And lo! even before pronouncing the sentence of their banishment from the earthly paradise, God speaks to them the first words of forgiveness and hope.

Instead of being cursed and driven out forever from the presence of their God, as were the rebel angels, they were to have a Redeemer; He it was Who would break the power won over them by the devil. And as their fall began by the prevarication of a woman, it was to be by the son of a woman that this redemption would be wrought. *Inimicitias ponam inter te et mulierem, et semen tuum et semen illius: ipsa conteret caput tuum.*

This has been named the "Protogospel," the first word of salvation. It is the first promise of redemption, the dawn of Divine mercy to the sinful earth, the first ray of that light which was one day to vivify the world, the first manifestation of the mystery hidden in God from all eternity.

Presently the nations, forgetful of the primeval revelations, sink insensibly into error. God then chooses for Himself a people that shall be the guardian of His promises. To this people God will, throughout the centuries, recall His promises, renew them, render them clearer and more abundant: this will be the era of the prophets.

If we listen to the sacred oracles of the prophets of Israel, we remark that the traits whereby God depicts the Person of the future Messias, and specifies the character of His mission, are at times so opposed that it seems as if they could not be encountered in the same person. Sometimes the prophets attribute to the Redeemer prerogatives such as could only befit a God, sometimes they predict for this Messias an overwhelming sum of humiliations, infirmities, and sufferings such as no one man could deserve.

This contrast so striking in the psalms of David is not less so in the prophecies of Isaias, the great Seer. So precise and full of detail is he, that he might be called the fifth Evangelist. One might think he was relating accomplished facts rather than foretelling future events.

The Prophet, transported up to heaven, says of the Messias: "Who shall declare His generation": *Generationem ejus quis enarrabit?* He gives Him names such as no man has ever borne: "His name shall be called Wonderful, Counsellor, God the mighty, the Father of the world to come, the Prince of Peace." Born of a Virgin, "His name shall be called *Emmanuel*," God with us. Isaias sees Him opening the eyes of the blind and unstopping the ears of the deaf, loosing the tongue of the dumb and making the lame to walk; he shows Him as "a Leader and a Master to the Gentiles"; he sees the idols utterly destroyed before Him, and he hears God promise by oath that "every knee shall be bowed" before this Saviour and every tongue shall confess His power.

And yet this Redeemer, Whose glory the prophet thus exalts, is to be overwhelmed with suffering, and such humiliations are to crush Him that He will be looked upon as "the most abject of men . . . as it were a leper, and as one struck by God and afflicted . . . led as a sheep to the slaughter . . . reputed with the wicked . . . because the Lord was pleased to bruise Him in infirmity."

In most of the prophets we see this opposition of traits wherewith they describe the greatness and the abasements, the power and the weakness, the sufferings and glory of the Messias. We see with what condescending wisdom God prepared the minds of His people to receive the revelation of the ineffable mystery of a God-Man at once the Supreme Lord Whom all nations adore, and the Victim for the sins of the World.

God thus willed to produce in the hearts of the just of the Old Covenant the requisite conditions whereby the coming of the Messias should be salutary for them. The more they were filled with faith and confidence in the promises announced by their prophets, the more they would burn with desire to see them realized, and the more they would be ready to receive the abundance of graces that the Saviour was to bring to the world.

All the Old Testament is a prolonged Advent, the prayers of which are summed up in this prayer of Isaias: "Send forth, O Lord, the Lamb, the Ruler of the earth. Drop down dew, ye heavens, from above, and let the clouds rain the just. Let the earth be opened, and bud forth a Saviour."

By a succession of marvels, Eternal Wisdom keeps intact, among the Chosen People, the ancient promises, unceasingly confirmed and developed by prophecy. The successive captivities of the sometimes unfaithful Jews serve to spread abroad the knowledge of these promises even among the Gentile nations, and meanwhile Eternal Wisdom likewise directs the destinies of these nations.

We know how during this long period of several centuries, God Who holds the hearts of kings in His hand, Whose power equals His wisdom, establishes and destroys one vast empire after another. To the empire of Nineveh, reaching as far as Egypt, follows that of Babylon. Then, as Isaias foretold, God "calls His servant Cyrus," king of the Persians and places the sceptre of Nabuchodonosor within his hands. After Cyrus, He makes Alexander the master of the nations, until finally He gives the world's empire to Rome, an empire of which the unity and peace is to serve the mysterious designs of the spread of the Gospel.

WHEN "the fulness of time" comes, God crowns all His preparations by the sending of St. John the Baptist, the last of the prophets, but greater than all, for God wills to make him His herald above all others, the very Forerunner of His beloved Son: *Propheta altissimi vocaberis.*

The other prophets only saw the Messias from afar off; he points Him out in person and in such clear terms that all sincere hearts understand: "Behold the Lamb of God, *Ecce Agnus Dei*, behold Him Who taketh away the sin of the world . . . there hath stood One in the midst of you

Whom you know not. The same is He that shall come after me, Who is preferred before me: the latchet of Whose shoe I am not worthy to loose. . . . I saw the Spirit coming down, as a dove from Heaven, and He remained upon Him . . . and I saw and gave testimony that this is the Son of God. . . ."

The Christ Whom John announced has come at last, the Light unto which John bore testimony. We ourselves have the happiness of believing in this Light "which enlighteneth every man that cometh into this world." We live moreover, in the blessed "fulness of time," and are not deprived, as were the Patriarchs, of seeing the reign of the Messias. Although we are not of those who beheld Christ in person and heard His words, we have the signal happiness of belonging to those nations of which David sang that they should be Christ's inheritance.

And yet the Holy Spirit Who governs the Church and is the first Author of our sanctification, wills that the Church should, year by year, consecrate four weeks in recalling to memory the long duration of the Divine preparations and that she should strive to place our souls in the interior attitude in which the faithful Jews lived whilst awaiting the advent of the Messias.

OUR Blessed Lady summed up in herself all the aspirations and longings of the human race awaiting the world's Saviour and God, whilst going far beyond them and giving them a value hitherto unattained. What holy intensity in her desires, what unshaken assurance in her confidence, what fervour in her love!

Let us humbly ask her to make us enter into her dispositions. She will hear our prayer. We shall have the immense joy of seeing Christ born anew within our hearts by the communication of more abundant grace, and we shall be enabled, like the Blessed Virgin, although in a lesser measure, to understand the truth of these words of St. John: "The Word was God . . . and the Word was made flesh, and dwelt among us, and we saw His glory . . . full of grace and truth. . . . And of His fulness we have all received, and grace for grace."

III

Christmastide

"O Admirabile Commercium!"

EACH one of Christ's mysteries is not only an historical fact which takes place in time, but moreover contains a special grace for the nourishment of our souls.

Now the special grace of the mystery of the Nativity, the fruit that we should gather from the contemplation of the Christ-Child is indicated by the Church herself at the Midnight Mass. After having offered the bread and wine which, in a few moments, are to be changed by the consecration into the Body and Blood of Jesus Christ, she sums up her desires in this prayer: "Grant, O Lord, that the oblation which we offer in today's festival may be acceptable unto Thee, and by Thy bountiful grace, through this most sacred intercourse, may we be found like unto Him in Whom is our substance united to Thee."

We ask to be partakers of that Divinity to which our humanity was united in the Person of Christ. It is like an exchange—a bargain. God, in becoming incarnate, takes our human nature and gives us in return a participation in His Divine Nature.

This thought, so concise in its form, is more explicitly

expressed in the Secret of the second Mass: "Grant, O Lord, that our offerings may be conformed to the mysteries of this day's Nativity, that as He Who is born as man is also God made manifest, so this earthly substance (which He unites to Himself) may confer upon us that which is divine."

Our offerings will be "conformed to the mysteries of this day's Nativity" if, by the contemplation of the Divine work at Bethlehem and the reception of the Eucharistic Sacrament, we participate in the eternal life which Christ wills to communicate to us through His Humanity.

LET us transport ourselves to the stable-cave at Bethlehem; let us behold the Child lying upon the straw. What is He in the sight of the profane, in the sight of an inhabitant of the little city who might happen to come there after the Birth of Jesus?

Only a new-born Babe to whom a woman of Nazareth had given birth; only a son of Adam like unto us, for His parents have Him inscribed upon the register of enrolment; the details of His genealogy can be followed. Many Jews saw nothing more in Him than this. Later on His compatriots, astonished at His wisdom, ask themselves where He could have learnt it, for, in their eyes, He had never been anything but "the son of a carpenter." *Nonne hic est fabri filius?*

But faith tells us that this Child is God's own Son. He is the Word, the Second Person of the Adorable Trinity; He is the Son Who receives Divine life from His Father, by an ineffable communication: *Sicut Pater habet vitam in semetipso sic dedit et Filio habere vitam in semetipso.* He possesses the Divine Nature with all its infinite perfections. In the heavenly splendours, *in splendoribus sanctorum*, God begets this Son by an eternal generation.

It is towards this Divine Sonship in the bosom of the Father that our adoration turns first of all; it is this Sonship that we extol in the Midnight Mass. At day-break, the Holy Sacrifice will celebrate Christ's Birth, according to the flesh: finally, the third Mass will be in honour of Christ's coming into our souls.

The Mass of Midnight, all enveloped with mystery, begins with these solemn words: *Dominus dixit ad me: Filius meus es tu, ego hodie genui te.* This cry that escapes from the soul of Christ united to the Person of the Word, reveals to earth for the first time, what the heavens hear from all eternity: "The Lord hath said to Me: Thou art My Son: this day have I begotten Thee." "This day" is the first of all the days of eternity, a day without dawn or decline.

The Heavenly Father now contemplates His Incarnate Son. The Word, although made Man, nevertheless remains God. Become the Son of Man, He is still the Son of God. The first glance that falls upon Christ, the first love wherewith He is surrounded, is the glance, the love of His Father. *Dilexit Me Pater.* What contemplation and what love! Christ is the Only-begotten Son of the Father: therein lies His essential glory. He is equal to and "consubstantial with the Father, God of God, Light of Light . . . by

Whom all things were made." It is of this Son that the words were spoken: "Thou in the beginning, O Lord, didst found the earth, and the works of Thy hands are the heavens. They shall perish, but Thou shalt continue; and they shall all grow old as a garment; and as a vesture shalt Thou change them, and they shall be changed; but Thou art the self-same, and Thy years shall not fail!"

And this "Word was made Flesh": *Et Verbum caro factum est.*

LET us contemplate this Infant lying in the manger. His eyes are closed, He sleeps, He does not outwardly manifest what He is. In appearance, He is only like all other infants, and yet, being God, being the Eternal Word, He is, at this moment, judging the souls that appear before Him. "He lies upon straw, and yet, as God, He sustains the universe and reigns in Heaven": *Jacet in præsepio et in cælis regnat.* This child, just beginning to grow, is the Eternal Whose Divine Nature knows no change. He Who is born in time is likewise He Who is before all time; He Who manifests Himself to the shepherds of Bethlehem is He Who, out of nothing, created the nations that "are before Him as if they had no being at all." If He needs a little milk to nourish Him, it is still by His hand that the birds of heaven are fed.

> *Parvoque lacte pastus est*
> *Per quem nec ales esurit.*[†]

† Hymn of Christmas Lauds.

To the eyes of faith there are two lives in this Babe; two lives indissolubly united in an ineffable manner, for the Human Nature belongs to the Word in such wise that there is but a single Person, that of the Word, Who sustains the Human Nature by His own Divine existence.

From whatever side our faith contemplates this wondrous exchange—*O admirabile commercium*—we see how admirable it is. Is not this childbearing of a Virgin indeed admirable! *Natus ineffabiliter ex virgine.* "A young Maiden has brought forth the King Whose Name is Eternal: to the honour of virginity she unites the joys of motherhood; before her, the like was never seen, nor shall it ever be so again."

What shall we say of the Blessed Virgin when she looked upon Jesus? Into what depths of the mystery did her gaze penetrate—that gaze so pure, so humble, so tender, so full of bliss? Who shall be able to express with what light the soul of Jesus inundated His Mother, and what perfect homage Mary rendered to her Son, to her God, to all the states and mysteries whereof the Incarnation is the substance and root!

When we contemplate the Incarnate Word at Bethlehem, let us rise above the things of sense that we may gaze upon Him with the eyes of faith alone. Faith makes us share even here below in the knowledge that the Divine Persons have of One Another. There is no exaggeration in this. Sanctifying grace makes us indeed partakers of the Divine nature. Now the activity of the Divine nature consists in the knowledge that the Divine Persons have One of the Other, and the love that they have One for the Other. We share therefore in this knowledge and in this love. And in the same way that sanctifying grace having its fruition in glory will give us the right of seeing God as He sees Himself, so upon earth, in the shadows of faith, grace gives us to see deep down into these mysteries through the eyes of God: *Lux tuæ claritatis infulsit.*

When our faith is intense and perfect we do not stay to look only at the outside of the mystery, but, passing through the Humanity, we penetrate even unto the Divinity which the Humanity at the same time hides and reveals. We behold Divine mysteries in the Divine light.

And ravished, astounded at such prodigious abasement, the soul, vivified by this faith, prostrates in adoration and yields herself entirely to procure the glory of a God Who, out of love for His creature, thus veils the native splendour of His unfathomable perfections. She can never rest until she has given all in return to fulfil her part in the exchange which He wills to contract with her, and until she has brought herself utterly into subjection to this "King of Peace Who comes with so much magnificence"† to save, sanctify, and, as it were, to deify her.

† Antiphon at Vespers on Christmas Day.

IV

The Epiphany

WHENEVER a soul comes into a more intimate contact with God, she feels herself wrapt round with mystery. This mystery is the inevitable consequence of the infinite distance separating the creature from the Creator. On all sides the finite being is surpassed by Him Who, everlastingly, is the plenitude of Being.

This is why one of the most profound characters of the Divine Being is His incomprehensibility. The invisibility here below of the Divine Light is a truly wonderful thing. "God is Light," says St. John, "and in Him is no darkness." But this light which bathes us all in its brightness, hides God instead of manifesting Him. It is with this light as with the sun; its very brilliancy prevents us from contemplating it.

And yet this light is the life of the soul. In Holy Scripture, the ideas of life and light are frequently associated. When the psalmist wants to describe the eternal beatitude whereof God is the source, he says that in God is the principle of life: *Quoniam apud Te est fons* VITÆ. And he immediately adds: "And in Thy light we shall see light." *Et in lumine Tuo* VIDEBIMUS LUMEN. In the same way Our Lord declares Himself to be "The Light of the world."

Again He says (and here is something more than a mere juxtaposition of words), "He that followeth Me walketh not in darkness, but shall have the light of life." And this light of life proceeds from the essential Life which is Light. Our life in Heaven will be to know the Eternal Light unveiled, and to rejoice in the splendour of this Light.

Already here below, God gives us a participation in this light by endowing the human soul with reason. Reason is a true light for man. All the natural activity of man, if he is to be worthy of himself, ought to be directed first of all by that light which shows him the good to be pursued, a light so powerful that it is even capable of revealing to man the existence of God and some of His perfections. St. Paul, writing to the faithful in Rome, declares the pagans to be inexcusable for not knowing God through contemplating the world, His handiwork. God's works contain a vestige, a reflection of His perfections, and thus, up to a certain point, they declare the Infinite Light.

THERE is another deeper, more merciful manifestation that God has made of Himself: this is the Incarnation.

The Divine Light, too dazzling to be manifested in all its splendour to our feeble sight, is veiled beneath the Sacred Humanity. "The brightness of eternal light," "Light shining forth from Light," *Lumen de Lumine*, has clad Himself in our flesh that through it we may contemplate the Divinity. Christ is God brought within our reach, showing Himself

to us in a life authentically human. The veil of the Humanity prevents the splendour of the Divinity from blinding
us, while for every soul of good-will, rays come forth
from this Man revealing that He is likewise God.

THIS manifestation of God to men is so extraordinary a
mystery, a work so full of mercy, constituting one of the
characters so essential to the Incarnation that, during the
first centuries, the Church had no special feast in honour
of the Saviour's birth at Bethlehem. She celebrated the
feast of the "Theophania," that is of the "Divine Manifesta-
tions" in the Person of the Incarnate Word. Herein was
included the manifestation of the Magi, the manifestation
upon the banks of the Jordan at the Baptism of Jesus, and
the manifestation at the marriage feast at Cana where
Christ wrought His first miracle. In passing from the
Church of the East to that of the West, the feast has
retained its name in Greek, *Epiphany*, the "manifestation,"
but it has almost exclusively for its object the manifestation of the Saviour to the Gentile world, the pagan
nations, in the person of the Magi.

GOD sends an angel to the shepherds, for the Chosen
People were accustomed to the apparition of the celestial
spirits; to the Magi, who study the stars, He causes a marvellous star to appear. This star is the symbol of the
inward illumination that enlightens souls in order to call
them to God.

The soul of every grown-up person is indeed enlightened, once at least, like the Magi, by the star of vocation to eternal salvation. The light is given to all. It is a dogma of our faith that God "will have all men to be saved."

Whatever was the country whence they came—Persia, Chaldea, Arabia, or India—the Magi, according to tradition, belonged to a priestly caste, and devoted themselves to the study of the stars. It is more than probable that they were not ignorant of the revelation made to the Jews of a King Who was to be their Deliverer and the Master of the world. The prophet Daniel, who had prophesied the time of His coming, had been in relation with their predecessors; perhaps even Balaam's prophecy that a star should "rise out of Jacob" was known to them. However that may be, behold now a wondrous star appears to them. Its extraordinary brightness attracting their gaze, awakens their attention, and at the same time an inward grace of illumination enlightens their souls. This grace prepares them to recognize the prerogatives of the One announced by the star; it inspires them to set out to seek Him in order to offer Him their homage.

The Magi's fidelity to the inspiration of grace is wonderful. Doubt takes no hold upon their minds; without staying to reason, they immediately begin to carry out their design. Neither the indifference nor the scepticism of those who surround them, nor the disappearance of the star, nor the difficulties belonging to an expedition of this kind, nor the length and dangers of the way stop them. They obey the Divine call without delay or hesitation. "We have seen His star in the East and are come."

THE lives of the Saints and the experience of souls show that there are often, in the supernatural life, decisive moments upon which depend all the value of our inner life, and sometimes even our eternity.

The Heavenly Father calls us to His Son by the inspiration of His grace. As soon as the star shines in our hearts, we should, like the Magi, instantly leave all: our sins, the occasions of sin, evil habits, infidelities, imperfections, attachment to creatures. Taking no account of criticism or the opinion of men, nor the difficulties of the work to be done, we should at once set out to seek Jesus. He wills this whether we have lost Him by mortal sin, or whether, already possessing Him by sanctifying grace, He calls us to a closer and more intimate union with Himself.

"*Vidimus stellam.* Lord, I have seen Thy star, and I come to Thee. What wilt Thou have me to do?"

THE marvellous star at length leads the Magi to the poor dwelling where they were at last to find Him Whom they have so long sought. They seek a King, a God, and they see only a Babe on His Mother's knee; not a Babe transfigured by Divine rays, as the Apostles were later to see the God-Man, but a weak little Child.

However, from this Little One so frail in appearance, a Divine power invisibly goes forth. He Who had made the star arise to lead the Magi to His cradle, now Himself enlightens them. He fills their minds with light and their hearts with love. And so it is that in this Child, they recognize their God.

The Gospel tells us nothing of their words, but it makes known to us the sublime act of their perfect faith: "And falling down they adored Him."

The attitude of adoration in the Magi translates the depth of their faith in eloquent language; the presents that they offer are likewise full of signification.

Gold, the most precious of metals, is the symbol of royalty; it denotes, on the other hand, the love and fidelity that everyone owes to his prince.

Incense is universally acknowledged to be the symbol of Divine worship: it is offered to God alone. In preparing this gift, the Magi showed that they intended to proclaim the Divinity of Him Whose Birth was announced by the star, and to confess this Divinity by the supreme adoration that can be given to God alone.

Finally, they had been inspired to bring Him myrrh. This gift of myrrh, used to dress wounds and embalm the dead, signified that Christ was Man, a Man capable of suffering, Who would one day die. It also symbolizes the spirit of penance and immolation which ought to characterize the life of disciples of the Crucified.

WE offer gold to Christ when, by a life full of love and fidelity to His commands, we proclaim that He is the

King of our hearts. We offer frankincense when we believe in His Divinity and confess it by our adoration and prayers. In uniting our humiliation and sufferings, our sorrows and tears to His, we bring Him myrrh.

Our Lord Himself supplies for what we lack. He is our riches, our thank-offering. He is, in His own Person, the perfect realization of all that is symbolized by the gifts of the Magi.

The Church knows so well this secret of God. On this day, when her mystical nuptials with Christ begin, she no longer offers to God gold, frankincense, and myrrh, but Him Who by these very gifts is represented, immolated upon the Altar and received into the hearts of His disciples.

Let us too beseech God in the words of the collect for the feast to grant that we, who already know Him by faith, may be brought to the contemplation of the beauty of His Majesty.

That will be the heavenly Epiphany.

V

Christ's Hidden Life

THE GOSPEL tells us that after having been found in the Temple, Jesus went down to Nazareth with His Mother and St. Joseph and there remained until He had reached the age of thirty years. And the sacred scribe sums up all this long period in these simple words: "And He was subject to them." *Et erat subditus illis.*

Thus out of a life of thirty-three years, Eternal Wisdom chose to pass thirty of these years in silence and obscurity, submission and labour.

Excepting those rays granted to a few privileged souls—the Shepherds, the Magi, Simeon, and Anna—the Light of the World is hidden thirty years, to be at last manifested only for the space of scarcely three years. Is not this mysterious? Is it not even disconcerting for our reason? If we had known the mission of Jesus, should we not have asked Him, as many of His kinsfolk did, to manifest Himself to the world?

But God's thoughts are not our thoughts, and His ways are higher than our ways. He Who comes to redeem the world wills to save it first of all by a life hidden from the world.

Truly, my Saviour, You are a hidden God: *Deus abscondi-tus Israel Salvator.* Doubtless, O Jesus, You grow "in wisdom, age, and grace with God and men." Your soul possesses the fulness of grace from the first moment of Your entrance into this world, and all the treasures of knowledge and wisdom, but this wisdom and grace are only manifested little by little. You remain a hidden God in the sight of men. Your Divinity is veiled beneath the outward appearance of a workman. O Eternal Wisdom, Who, in order to draw us out of the abyss into which Adam's proud disobedience had plunged us, chose to dwell in a humble workshop therein to obey creatures, I adore and bless You.

In the sight of His contemporaries the existence of Jesus Christ at Nazareth appears to be like the ordinary existence of a simple artisan. Later, when Christ reveals Himself in His public life, the Jews of His part of the country are so astonished at His wisdom and His words, at the sublimity of His doctrine and the greatness of His works, that they ask each other: "How came this man by His wisdom and miracles? Is not this the carpenter's son? Is not His Mother called Mary? . . . whence therefore hath He all these things?" Christ was a stumbling block for them.

This mystery of the hidden life contains teachings which our faith ought eagerly to gather up.

First of all there is nothing great in God's sight except that which is done for His glory, through the grace of

Christ. We are only acceptable to God according to the measure wherein we are like unto His Son Jesus.

Christ's Divine Sonship gives infinite value to His least actions; He is not less adorable nor less pleasing to His Father when He wields the chisel and plane than when He dies upon the Cross to save mankind. In us, sanctifying grace, which makes us God's adopted children, deifies all our activity in its root and renders us worthy, like Jesus, although by a different title, of His Father's complacency.

Sanctifying grace is the first source of our true greatness. It confers upon our life, however commonplace it may seem, its true nobility and imperishable splendour.

Oh, if we knew the gift of God!

BUT this gift is hidden.

The Kingdom of God is built up in silence; it is, before all things, interior and hidden in the depths of the soul: *Vita vestra est abscondita cum Christo in Deo.* Undoubtedly grace possesses a virtue which nearly always overflows in works of charity but the principle of its powers is entirely within. It is in the depths of the heart that the true intensity of the Christian life lies, it is there that God dwells, adored and served by faith, recollection, humility, obedience, simplicity, labour, and love.

Our outward activity has no stability nor supernatural fruitfulness save in so far as it is linked to this interior life. We shall truly only bear fruit outwardly according to the degree of the supernatural intensity of our inner life.

What can we do greater here below than promote Christ's reign within souls? We shall, however, succeed in this work by no other means than those employed by our Divine Head. Let us be thoroughly convinced that we shall do more for the good of the Church, the salvation of souls, the glory of our Heavenly Father, in seeking first of all to remain united to God by a life of love and faith, of which He alone is the object, than by a devouring and feverish activity which leaves us no leisure to find Him again in solitude, recollection, prayer, and self-detachment.

Nothing favours this intense union of the soul with God like the hidden life. And this is why souls living the inner life, and enlightened from on high, love to contemplate the life of Jesus at Nazareth. They find in it a special charm and, moreover, abundant graces of holiness.

IT is especially through the Blessed Virgin Mary that we shall obtain a share in the graces that Christ merited for us by His hidden life at Nazareth, for it must have been for the Mother of God a well-spring of priceless graces. We are dazzled by the very thought of them, and intuitions scarcely to be expressed in words are awakened within us when we reflect what those thirty years must have been for her.

Certainly there must have been much that was incomprehensible even for the Blessed Virgin. No one could live in continual contact, as she did, with the Infinite, without at times feeling and touching mystery. But yet what abundant light for her soul, what a continual increase of love this ineffable intercourse with a God, working under her eyes, must have wrought in her most pure heart!

Mary lived with Jesus in a union surpassing all that can be said of it. They were truly one; the mind, heart, soul—the whole existence of Our Lady were in absolute accord with the mind, heart, soul, and life of her Son. Her life was, as it were, a pure and perfect vibration, tranquil and full of love, of the very life of Jesus.

The Blessed Virgin merited the joys of Divine Motherhood by her faith and love, and Jesus wishes to teach us that we may share, certainly not in the glory of having given birth to Him, but the joy of bringing Him forth in souls. And how are we to obtain this joy? In hearing and keeping the word of God. We hear it by faith, we keep it by doing through love what it ordains.

Such is for us, as for Mary, the source of the soul's true joy and the way of happiness. If, after having inclined our heart to the teaching of Jesus, we obey His will and remain united to Him, we shall become as dear to Him— it is He Himself Who declares it—as if we were for Him a mother, brother, sister. What closer union than this could we desire?

VI

The Baptism and Temptation of Jesus

T HE MYSTERIES of the Birth and Childhood of Jesus are marked by contrasts of shadow and light which make our faith "reasonable," whilst leaving it free. We shall find this supernatural dispensation again in the events wherewith Christ, after the thirty years of His Hidden Life enters upon His Public Life; namely, His Baptism by John the Forerunner in the waters of the Jordan and his temptation in the desert.

AFTER a life given up to austerity, and when he was in about his thirtieth year, John, urged by divine inspiration, began his teaching upon the banks of the Jordan. All his teaching was summed up in these words: "Do penance, for the kingdom of heaven is at hand." To these urgent exhortations he joined baptism in the river, thereby to show his hearers the necessity of purifying their souls in order to render them less unworthy of the Saviour's coming. This baptism was only conferred on those who acknowledged themselves to be sinners and confessed their faults.

Now, one day when the Precursor administered "baptism for the remission of sins," Christ Jesus, Whose hour had come to leave the obscurity of the hidden life and to manifest the Divine secrets to the world, mingled with the multitude of sinners and came with them to receive from John the purifying ablution.

When we ponder on this thought that He Who thus proclaims Himself a sinner and voluntarily presents Himself to receive the baptism of penance is the Second Person of the Blessed Trinity, before Whom the angels veil their faces, singing "Holy, holy, holy," we are confounded at such a prodigious abasement.

When John, enlightened from on high, recognizes in Him the Son of God of Whom He had said: "The same is He Who shall come after me . . . the latchet of Whose shoe I am not worthy to loose," he refuses with all his might to confer upon Christ the baptism of penance. "I ought to be baptized by Thee, and comest Thou to me?" But Christ replies: "Suffer it to be so now. For so it becometh us to fulfil all justice."

What is this justice? It is the humiliation of the adorable Humanity of Jesus, which, in rendering supreme homage to Infinite Holiness, constitutes the full payment of all our debts towards Divine Justice. Jesus, just and innocent, takes the place of all our sinful race, and by His immolation becomes "the propitiation for our sins and . . . for those of the whole world." It is thus that He fulfils all justice.

"AND Jesus being baptized, forthwith came out of the water; and lo, the heavens were opened to Him: and He saw the Spirit of God descending as a dove, and coming upon Him. And behold a voice from heaven, saying: This is My beloved Son, in Whom I am well pleased."

Jesus stoops so low as to mingle with the multitude of sinners, and forthwith the heavens are opened to magnify Him—He asks for the baptism of penance, of reconciliation, and behold the Spirit of Love testifies that He abides in Jesus with the plenitude of His gifts of grace—He acknowledges Himself worthy of the strokes of Divine Justice, and the Father declares that He takes His delight in Him.

The mission of Jesus has a double aspect: it bears at the same time the character of redemption and of sanctification. It is to redeem souls and then to infuse life into them. That is the whole work of the Saviour. These two elements are inseparable but distinct. Therefore this mystery of the Baptism of Jesus, which marks the beginning of His public life, contains as it were the summary of His mission here below.

Baptism, with faith in Jesus Christ, has become for us the Sacrament of Divine adoption and Christian initiation.

It is in the Name of the Blessed Trinity revealed to us on the banks of the Jordan, that baptism is conferred upon us.

In the same way as baptism constituted the summary of all Christ's mission, at once redeeming and sanctifying, so baptism contains for us, in germ, the whole Christian life with its double aspect of "death to sin" and "life unto God."

So true is it that "as many . . . as have been baptized in Christ, have put on Christ," so true is it that we make but one with Jesus in all His mysteries!

Scarcely was Jesus baptized, the Gospel tells us, than He was led by the Spirit into the desert. The sacred writers use different expressions to signify the action of the Holy Spirit. According to St. Mark, Jesus was "driven." What does this term signify if not the vehemence of the Holy Spirit's action over the soul of Christ. And to what end was He thus driven into the desert? "To be tempted by the devil."

IN order to understand the depths of this mystery we must first of all recall the place that temptation holds in our spiritual life.

The Divine perfections exact that every free, rational creature shall be subjected to trial before being admitted to enjoy future beatitude. It is needful that, standing in God's sight, this creature shall freely renounce all self-satisfaction, choosing rather to acknowledge God's sovereignty and obey His law. God's sanctity and justice demand this homage.

This choice, glorious for the Infinite Being, is for us the foundation of the merit which God rewards with heavenly beatitude. The Council of Trent has declared that it is God Who saves us, but in such a way that salvation shall be at the same time a gift of His mercy and the reward of our merits. Eternal life will be our recompense because, having had to choose, we resisted temptation in order to cleave to God.

The first man was subjected to trial, he faltered, he fell away, preferring his own satisfaction to God. He drew all his race into his rebellion, his fall, and his chastisement.

It was necessary that the second Adam, Who represented all the predestined, should act in a directly contrary manner. In His adorable wisdom, God the Father willed that Christ Jesus, our Head and our Model, should be placed in the face of temptation, and, by His free choice, come forth victorious.

LET us contemplate our Divine Captain in combat with the prince of the rebellious spirits. We know that Jesus remained forty days and nights in the desert, in the midst of the beasts, in complete solitude and fasting. Our Lord did not will to work a miracle to prevent in Himself the effects of this fast, and indeed after so prolonged a lapse of time He must have been in a state of extreme exhaustion. The devil took occasion of this to tempt Him.

Although sharing in our infirmities and weakness, Christ's Sacred Manhood cannot know sin nor be subject to any ignorance, error, nor moral weakness. The temptation that Christ can undergo does not touch His soul and remains wholly exterior; He can be tempted only by "principalities and powers . . . the rulers of the world of this darkness . . . the spirits of wickedness."

As the Gospel tells us, the tempter approaches Jesus: *Et accedens tentator.* And seeing Him in a state of exhaustion, he seeks to make him fall into a sin of gluttony. Not a sin of great gluttony by presenting Christ with savoury food—the devil had too high an opinion of the One Whom he attacked to believe that He would succumb to a suggestion of that kind—but He represents to Jesus, faint with hunger, that if He be the Son of God, He has power of working a miracle to satisfy this hunger. Therefore he tries to urge Christ to advance the hour of His Father by performing a prodigy of which the end was altogether personal.

Seeing himself repulsed, the devil understands that he has before him, if not the Son of God, at least a being of great holiness. Thus he sets about employing a more dangerous weapon. He knows human nature wonderfully; he knows that those who have attained a high degree of perfection, and of union with God, are above the reach of the gross appetites of the senses, but can be seduced by more subtle suggestions of pride and presumption; they can believe themselves to be better than others and think that, if they voluntarily expose themselves to danger, God owes them an altogether special protection on account of their fidelity. The devil, therefore, tries to tempt Christ in this way. Making use of his spiritual power, he transports Jesus upon the pinnacle of the temple and says to Him: "If Thou be the Son of God, cast Thyself down, for it is written: That He hath given His Angels charge over thee, and in their hands they shall bear thee up, lest perhaps thou dash thy foot upon a stone." If Jesus be the Son of God what a wonderful sign of His messianic mission, what an evident proof of God being with Him, if He were to appear from on high and thus descend in the midst of the multitude thronging the courts of the temple! And to render his suggestion more seductive the devil employs the divine word to support it. . . . This time again the devil is defeated. The Word of God triumphs over his snares.

The spirit of darkness endeavours to vanquish Christ in a last assault. Taking Him upon a high mountain he shows Him all the kingdoms of the world, and displays before His eyes all their riches, splendour, and glory. What a temptation for the ambition of one believing himself to be the Messias! But a price has to be paid for this: "All this will I give thee, if falling down thou wilt adore me." We know the response of Jesus and with what vigour He repulses the sacrilegious suggestion of the Evil One.

The prince of darkness now knows himself to be entirely unmasked. There is nothing left him but to withdraw. However the Gospel says that the devil departed from Jesus only for a time: *Usque ad tempus.* The sacred writer indicates by this that during the public life the devil will make other attempts. The Saviour's death upon the Cross was to be the decisive stroke whereby to overthrow the devil's empire. . . .

IF Christ, the Word Incarnate, the Son of God, willed to

enter into combat with the evil spirit shall we be astonished if the members of the Mystical Body must follow the same path? So many, even pious people, believe temptation to be a sign of reprobation. But most often it is the contrary. Having become disciples of Jesus by Baptism, we cannot be above our Divine Master.

Yes, the devil can tempt us, and tempt us mightily and just when we think that we are the most secure from his shafts—at time of prayer, or after Holy Communion; yes, even at those blessed moments he can whisper thoughts against faith, against hope; he can urge us to a spirit of independence and revolt against the rights of God; he can raise up evil passions in us. He can, and he will not fail to do so.

Once more, do not let us be surprised; let us not forget that Christ was tempted before us, and not only tempted, but touched by the spirit of darkness. He permitted the devil to lay a hand upon His most Sacred Humanity. Neither let us forget that it was not only as the Son of God that Jesus overcame the devil, but likewise as Head of the Church. In Him and by Him we have triumphed and still triumph over the suggestions of the rebel spirit.

The grace that the Incarnate Word merited for us in undergoing temptation is the grace of strength to defeat the devil in our turn, to come forth victorious from the conflict through which we must necessarily pass before being admitted to enjoy divine life in the blessedness of Heaven.

Christ Jesus has merited that those who are united to Him shall share—and share according to their union with Him—in this impeccability.

We here approach the very centre of the mystery.

We see in the Gospel that Christ was impeccable, inaccessible to the evil of sin, to the least imperfection. But what is the source of this moral invulnerability?

It is the fundamental truth that He is the very Son of God. As the Second Person of the Blessed Trinity, He is infinite Holiness and cannot succumb to evil.

However the Humanity of Jesus in itself is a human nature created like unto our own. Union with the Divinity did not exempt it from those weaknesses which are compatible with the state of Son of God. Christ suffers hunger and thirst. Fear, sadness, weariness, take real possession of His soul, and yet there is not the shadow of an imperfection in him. If then Christ's Human Nature, *as such*, enjoys impeccability it is because it is strengthened in holiness in a marvellous way.

Now the means that God uses in order to render the blessed soul of Jesus inaccessible to moral evil, so as to establish it in impeccability, is to place Him under the protection of the Most High, *in adjutorio Altissimi*, or, according to the more significant rendering of the original text, "In the secret sanctuary of the Divinity": *In sanctuario secreto divinitatis.* And this sanctuary is the Beatific Vision.

As we know, the Beatific Vision is the blessed contemplation of God as He is in Himself. They to whom this grace is granted can never more separate themselves from God, because they *see* that God is the Supreme Good, and that no particular good, however vast it be, can be compared to Him. Hence sin, which consists in turning away from the law of God and from His will, or, what comes to the same thing, in turning away from God Himself, to attach oneself to some good as seen in self or the creature, is rendered practically impossible. In this blessed state wherein the intellect contemplates the Very Truth, there is no room for any ignorance, illusion, or error; and the will, cleaving to the absolute Good that contains the plenitude of all good, knows neither hesitation, nor falling away, nor defection of any kind. The soul that reaches this summit is, in theological language, perfectly "confirmed in grace."

HERE below, it is not given to us to abide perfectly in this "Sanctuary of the Divinity." It is faith that takes the place of the Beatific Vision for us upon earth. Through faith, we have God ever present. This faith, in the light of which we walk, is the source of union with Jesus and the root of perfection. In the measure whereby, through faith, a soul lives in the contemplation of God, and remains united to Jesus Christ, she becomes invulnerable to temptation.

God takes His delight in such a soul. He protects her; He renders her, little by little, invulnerable. All her enemies may attack her, a thousand shall fall at her side, and ten thousand at her right hand, and they shall not come nigh her. She will tread the devils underfoot; all the universe may rise up and be let loose against her, she will say to God: "Thou art my Protector and my Refuge," and He will deliver her from all snares and dangers.

Our Mother, the Church, who is full of solicitude for her children, knows to what perils they are exposed. She knows, on the other hand, what powerful life-giving graces are granted to us through the mysteries of the Incarnate Word and through our union with Him, and so she recalls to us each year at the beginning of Lent the mystery of the temptation of Jesus.

At the same time she places upon our lips the whole 90th psalm, which begins with the words: "He that dwelleth in the sanctuary of the Divinity shall abide under the protection of the God of Heaven." It is pre-eminently the psalm of confidence in the midst of struggle, trial, and temptation.

VII

Some Aspects of
the Public Life of Jesus

THE APOSTLE St. John says at the close of his Gospel: "There are also many other things which Jesus did; which, if they were written everyone, the world itself, I think, would not be able to contain the books that should be written."

This thought is brought home to us in a special manner as we are about to contemplate our Lord's public life. If we would comment in detail upon each of His recorded words and actions a whole lifetime would not suffice.

We will at least take some characteristic points from this period of the Saviour's life.

When we read the Gospel we see that Christ speaks and acts not only as man, like unto us, but also as God, high above all creatures. If as Man, born of Mary, He is the Son of David, He is also the Lord, seated at the right hand of God, sharing His eternal power and infinite glory.

Thus He declares Himself to be the Supreme Lawgiver, by the same title as God. As God gave the Law to Moses, so Christ establishes the code of the Gospel. "You have heard that it was said to them of old . . . but I say to you. . . ." This is the formula that is repeated throughout the Sermon on the Mount. He shows Himself to be the sovereign Master of the Law to such a degree that He derogates from it by His own authority when He so pleases, with an entire independence, as being He Who instituted it.

This power is boundless. Jesus forgives sins, a privilege which God alone enjoys, because it is God alone Whom sin offends. "Be of good heart, son, thy sins are forgiven thee," He says to the man sick of the palsy. The Pharisees, scandalized at hearing a man speak thus, murmur among themselves. "Who can forgive sins, but God alone." But Jesus reads the secret thoughts of their hearts, and to prove that He possesses this divine power, not by delegation but as being personally entitled to it, He immediately works a miracle: "That you may know that the Son of man hath power on earth to forgive sins, (then said He to the man sick of the palsy), Arise, take up thy bed, and go into thy house."

This is a characteristic example. Christ Jesus works miracles by His own authority. Except before the raising of Lazarus, when He asks His Father that the miracle He is about to perform may enlighten those who are to witness it, He never prays before manifesting His power, as did the prophets; but with a word, a gesture, a single act of the will, He heals the maimed, makes the paralysed walk, multiplies the loaves, calms the furious waves, casts out devils, raises the dead.

It is above all in St. John's Gospel that we find upon the lips of Jesus testimonies to a union between Himself and His Father such as can only be explained by the Divine nature that He indivisibly possesses with the Father and their common Spirit.

Except when He teaches His disciples how to pray, Jesus Christ never says: "Our Father." Always when speaking of His relations with God He says "the Father, My Father," and in speaking to His disciples, "your Father." Our Lord is careful to denote the essential difference existing in this matter between Himself and other men: He is the Son of God by nature, they are so only by adoption.

This Son Who is Jesus is so great and His Sonship so ineffable that only the Father, Who is God, can know Him; the Father is of such majesty, His Fatherhood is so sublime a mystery, that the Son alone can know what the Father is.

The great mission of Jesus, above all during His public life, is to manifest His Divinity to the world. All His teaching, all His miracles, tend to inculcate this truth. Doubtless He only inculcates this truth gradually in consideration of the Jews' monotheistic notions; but with admirable wisdom, He makes all converge towards the manifestation of His Divine Sonship. At the end of His life, when upright minds are sufficiently prepared, He does not hesitate to confess His Divinity before His judges, at the peril of His life. Jesus is the King of Martyrs, of all those who, by the shedding of their blood, have professed their faith in His Divinity.

This faith in His Son's Divinity is, according to Jesus' own words, the work that God especially demands of us: *Hoc est opus Dei, ut credatis in eum quem misit ille.*

It is this faith that brings healing to many who are sick with divers diseases: *Secundum fidem vestram fiat vobis*; to Magdalen it brings the forgiveness of her sins: *Fides tua te salvam fecit vade in pace.* It is this faith whereby Peter merits to be established as the indestructible foundation of the Church; it is this faith which makes the Apostles pleasing to the Father, and the objects of His love: *Pater amat vos, quia vos me amastis, et credidistis.* Faith in Jesus Christ, the eternal Son of God, is the basis of our whole spiritual life, the deep root of all justification, the essential condition of all progress, the certain means of attaining the summit of all sanctity.

If Christ reveals to the world the dogma of His eternal filiation, it is by means of His Humanity that He reveals and manifests to us the perfections of His Divine Nature. Although He be the true Son of God, He loves to call Himself "the Son of Man." He gives Himself this title even on the most solemn occasions when He claims with most authority the prerogatives of the Divine Being.

Indeed each time that we come in contact with Him, we are in the presence of this sublime mystery, namely, the union of two natures, divine and human, in one and the same Person, without mingling or confusion of natures, without division of person. This is the initial mystery that we ought ever to have before our eyes when we contemplate Our Lord. Each of His mysteries brings before us either the oneness of His adorable Person, or the truth of His Divine Nature, or the reality of His human condition.

One of the principal and most touching aspects of the economy of the Incarnation is the manifestation of the Divine perfections made to mankind through the Human Nature. God's attributes, His eternal perfections are incomprehensible to us here below; they surpass our understanding. But, in becoming Man, the Incarnate Word reveals to the simplest minds the inaccessible perfections of His Divinity, by the words which fall from His human lips and by the actions performed by His human nature. We are charmed and drawn to Him as He enables us to grasp these divine perfections by His visible actions.

Of all the Divine perfections, love is certainly the one that the Incarnate Word is most pleased to reveal to us.

The human heart needs a tangible love in order to realize something of infinite love. Nothing, indeed, so much attracts our poor hearts as to contemplate Christ Jesus, true God as well as true Man, translating the eternal goodness into human deeds. When we see Him lavishly scattering around Him treasures of compassion and mercy, we are enabled to conceive something of that ocean of Divine kindness whence these treasures have their inexhaustible source.

We see with what condescension, at times surprising, our Saviour stoops towards human misery under every form, sin included. And never let it be forgotten that even when He stoops towards us, He remains the very Son of God, God Himself, the Almighty Being, Infinite Wisdom, Who, ordering all things in truth, does nothing save what is sovereignly perfect. This undoubtedly gives to the words of kindness that He utters, to the deeds of mercy that He performs, an inestimable value.

Indeed Jesus reveals Himself to all as a King full of meekness and kindness. We should need to quote every page of the Gospel to show how misery, weakness, infirmity, and suffering have the gift of touching Him and in so irresistible a manner that He can refuse them nothing. St. Luke is careful to note how He is "moved with compassion": *Misericordia motus.* The blind and the lame, deaf-mutes, the palsy-stricken and lepers, come to Him, and the Gospel says that He "healed all": *Sanabat omnes.*

He welcomes them all with unwearying gentleness. He allows Himself to be pressed on all sides; one day He cannot "so much as eat bread." Behold how at Naim He meets a poor widow following the mortal remains of her only son. Jesus sees her, He sees her tears; His Heart, deeply touched, cannot bear this sorrow: "O woman, weep not!" *Noli flere!* And at once He commands death to give up its prey.

The deepest form of misery is sin. If there is a trait particularly striking in the conduct of the Incarnate Word during His public life it is the strange preference that He manifests for His ministry towards sinners.

The sacred writers tell us that "as He was sitting at meat . . . behold many publicans and sinners came and sat down with Jesus and His disciples." Jesus was even called "the friend of publicans and sinners," and when the Pharisees showed that they were scandalized at this, Jesus, far from denying the fact, confirmed it, giving the reason that lay at the root: "They that are well have no need of a physician, but they that are sick. For I came not to call the just but sinners."

In the Eternal Plan, Jesus is our Elder Brother. He has taken our nature, sinful in the race, but pure in His Person. He knows that the great mass of mankind falls into sin and needs forgiveness; He knows that souls sitting "in the darkness and in the shadow of death" do not understand the direct revelation of Divine things and that they can only be drawn to the Father by the condescension of the Sacred Manhood.

IN the Sermon on the Mount, Christ astonished the Jewish audience by the revelation of a doctrine that ran counter to their inveterate instincts and worldly prejudices. He declared before them all that the blessed of His Kingdom are the poor of spirit, the meek, those that mourn, those that hunger and thirst after justice. He declared that the merciful, the clean of heart, the peacemakers are the true children of His Heavenly Father, and that the greatest of the Beatitudes is to be an object of persecution for His sake.

This doctrine which forms the Gospel's "great charter" of the poor, the little, the humble, is the antithesis of that which the Pharisees preached by words and example, and we hear Our Saviour pronounce against them a series of eight maledictions forming the counterpart of the eight Beatitudes.

We see with what indignation Christ, the infallible Truth and the Life of souls, warns the multitude, and His disciples in particular, against a teaching and conduct that turned men away from the Kingdom of God, distorted the truth and precepts of the Law, established a wholly exterior religion, merely surface purity under which corruption and persecuting hatred were concealed.

What a contrast between the terrible denunciations heaped upon the Pharisees and Our Lord's attitude towards the greatest sinners, the Samaritan woman, the Magdalen, the woman taken in adultery whom He forgives without a word of reproach, and towards malefactors, such as the Good Thief to whom He promises Paradise.

Whence comes this difference? It is because every form of weakness or of misery, when humbly acknowledged, draws forth the compassion of His Heart and the mercy of His Father, whilst pride, especially intellectual pride, like to the sin of the demons, excites His indignation; and the pharisaical spirit is the epitome of all that is odious and hypocritical in pride, besides substituting a formalism of human origin for the eternal law of God.

The devil has no more redoubtable nor fatal snare than that of making some form of pharisaism pass for the holiness required by the Gospel. In this way the prince of darkness attacks even souls seeking after perfection. We see how important it is not to base our holiness upon such and such a practice of devotion, however excellent, which we choose for ourselves, nor upon such and such an observance of our religious rule. Such an observance may be suspended by a higher law as is, for instance, the law of charity towards our neighbour. Holiness for us must be based upon the fulfilment of the divine law, the natural law, the precepts of the decalogue, the commandments of the Church, and the duties of our state. A piety that does not respect this hierarchy of duties ought to be held suspect; all asceticism that is not governed by the precepts and doctrine of the Gospel cannot come from the Holy Spirit Who inspired the Gospel.

Our fidelity must not be bounded by the letter but have its source in love and be supported by confidence in a Saviour full of kindness. Then, whatever be our weaknesses, our miseries, our shortcomings, and the faults that escape us, the day will dawn when we shall for ever bless the One Who appeared upon earth under a human form. He came to heal our diseases, to redeem us from sin's abyss; it is again He Who will crown us forever with the gifts of His mercy and love.

VIII

The Mystery
of the Transfiguration

Second Sunday in Lent

THE CHURCH makes us read the Gospel narrative of the Transfiguration twice: on the second Sunday in Lent in order to encourage us to do penance by the distant perspective of the glory that Christ promises us in His Transfiguration, and again on August 6th, in honour of the manifestation of Christ's Divine splendour on Mount Thabor.

Nothing ought to be dearer to us than the dogma of the Divinity of Jesus: first of all because nothing is more pleasing to Him, and secondly because this dogma is at once the foundation, centre, and crown of our whole inner life. . . .

It is the last year of Our Lord's public life. Until now He has only made very rare allusions to His future Passion; but, says St. Matthew "from that time Jesus began to show to His disciples that He must go to Jerusalem, and suffer many things from the ancients and scribes and chief priests, and be put to death, and the third day rise again."

Soon after this prediction, our Divine Saviour takes

with Him the three Apostles of predilection: Peter, upon whom a few days before He had promised to found His Church; James, who was to be the first martyr of the Apostolic College: and John, the disciple of love. Christ Jesus had already chosen them to be witnesses of the raising of Jairus' daughter; now He leads them upon a high mountain to witness a still greater manifestation of His Divinity. Tradition sees Mount Thabor in this "high mountain." Isolated, it rises at the distance of some leagues to the east of Nazareth. It is covered with a rich vegetation. From its summit, the view extends in every direction.

It is here, upon this height, far distant from the sounds of earth, that Jesus goes with His disciples. And, according to His custom, He enters into prayer, and whilst He prays, He is transfigured. His countenance shines like the sun, His raiment becomes white as snow; He is surrounded with a divine atmosphere.

When Jesus begins to pray, His disciples fall asleep; but presently the dazzling light awakens them; they behold Him resplendent and at His side are Moses and Elias, talking with Him. And Peter is filled with such joy at the sight of the Master's glory that, beside himself, not knowing what he says, he cries out: "Master, it is good for us to be here. *Bonum est nos hic esse.* It is good to be here with Thee; it is good that this should be the end of the conflict with the Pharisees, and the snares laid by them, the end of weariness and journeyings and humiliations. Let us stay here. We will make three tents, one for Thee, one for

Moses, one for Elias, and as for us we will dwell with Thee."

While Peter is thus speaking, a bright cloud overshadows them, and a voice comes out of this cloud saying: "This is My beloved Son, in Whom I am well pleased, hear ye Him." Immediately filled with awe and reverence, the Apostles throw themselves down in adoration before God.

But Jesus touches them and says: "Arise, and fear not." They, lifting up their eyes, see "no one but only Jesus." They see Jesus as they had seen Him a short time before when they ascended the mountain with Him, the same Jesus Whom they were accustomed to see—Jesus, the Son of the carpenter of Nazareth, Jesus Who before long was to die upon a cross.

The disciples did not perhaps at this moment penetrate into all the depths of the mystery of which they were the privileged witnesses. It was enough for them to be armed in advance against the scandal of the Cross. This is why Jesus forbade them to speak of this vision.

Later, after the Resurrection, when on the day of Pentecost the Holy Spirit had confirmed them in their dignity as apostles, they revealed, by the voice of Peter, the splendours they had contemplated. Peter, the visible head of the Church, he who had received from the Incarnate Word the mission of confirming his brethren in the faith, announces how the majesty of Jesus had been revealed to him, and how "Jesus received from God the Father, honour and glory . . . when we were with Him in the Holy Mount." Peter, the supreme Pastor, recalls this vision in order to exhort the faithful, and us with them, not to waver in the faith.

For it was likewise for us that the Transfiguration took place. The disciples chosen to witness it, says St. Leo, represent the whole Church; it is to her, as well as to the Apostles, that the Father speaks in declaring the Divinity of His Son Jesus and in bidding us hear Him. When He tells us that Jesus is His beloved Son, the Father reveals to us His life; and when we believe in this revelation we participate in the knowledge of God Himself. The Father knows the Son in endless glory; as for us, we know Him in the shadows of faith whilst awaiting the light of eternity.

The collect for the Feast tells us that our adoption as children of God was wondrously signified by the Divine Voice from the shining cloud.

The Eternal Father makes known to us that Jesus is His Son, but, as we know, Jesus is likewise "the Firstborn amongst many brethren." Having taken a human nature, He makes us partakers, by His grace, of His Divine Sonship. If He is God's own Son by nature, we are so by grace. Jesus is one of ourselves through His Incarnation; He makes us like to Him by bestowing upon us a participation in His Divinity, so that we may make with Him but one Mystical Body. That is the Divine adoption: *Ut filii Dei nominemur et simus.*

In declaring that Jesus is His Son, the Father declares that those who, by grace, are partakers of His Divinity are equally, although by another title, His children. It is through Jesus, the Incarnate Word, that this adoption is given to us. And in adopting us as His children, the Father gives us the right of one day sharing His Divine and glorious life. That is the "perfect adoption": *Adoptio perfecta*.

In the Transfiguration we see the revelation of our future greatness. This glory which surrounds Jesus is to become our portion because He gives to us, His members, the right of sharing in the inheritance that He possesses as the very Son of God.

Here below we are, by grace, God's children, but "it hath not yet appeared what we shall be" one day in consequence of this adoption. That day will come when the lightnings having enlightened the world, and the voice of judgment having made the earth shake and tremble to its foundations, the just, according to Our Lord's own words, shall "shine as the sun in the kingdom of their Father." Their bodies will be glorious like unto Christ's body upon Thabor; it is the same glory which shines upon the Humanity of the Incarnate Word that will transfigure our bodies.

Doubtless we ought not to believe that Christ upon the Holy Mount had all the glory wherewith His Manhood is now resplendent in Heaven; it was but a reflection of that glory and yet it was so dazzling that the disciples were ravished. This wondrous radiance was an overflowing of the Divinity upon the Humanity, an irradiance from the furnace of eternal life. It was not a borrowed light, coming from without, but rather a reflection of that incommensurable majesty which Christ contained within Himself. For love of us, Jesus, during His earthly life, habitually hid the divine life under the veil of mortal flesh. The continuous light would have blinded our feeble eyes, but now at the Transfiguration He allowed it to throw its splendour upon the Humanity which He had taken.

To be the child of the Eternal Father, to attain the perfect and glorious adoption, we have but to listen to Jesus.

He speaks to us in the Gospel, He speaks to us by the voice of the Church, by that of events and trials, and by the inspiration of His Spirit. But in order to listen well, silence is needful. We should often, like Jesus at the Transfiguration, go apart into a solitary place. Certainly, Jesus is to be found everywhere, even in the turmoil of great cities, but He is only heard well in a peaceful soul surrounded by an atmosphere of prayer and silence.

If the soul is closed to earth's clamours, to the tumult of the passions and senses, the Incarnate Word Himself will little by little become Master of it. He will make us understand that true joys, the deepest joys, are those that are found in His service. The soul that has the happiness of being admitted, like the privileged Apostles, into the Divine Master's intimacy will sometimes feel constrained to cry out with St. Peter, "Lord, it is good for us to be here": *Domine, bonum est nos hic esse.*

Doubtless, Jesus does not always lead us to Thabor,

there where "it is good to be." He does not always give us sensible consolations; if He does give them, we ought not to reject them, for they come from Him. We must accept them humbly, but without seeking them for themselves and without being attached to them. As long as we are here below it is much more often to Calvary that Jesus leads us, that is to say through disappointments, trials, and temptations.

What did Jesus speak of when He was upon the mountain with Moses and Elias? Of His Divine prerogatives, of His glory which transported His disciples? No, but of His approaching Passion, of the excess of His sufferings. It is by the cross that Christ leads us to life and, because He knows that we are weak in time of trial, He willed to show us by His Transfiguration what glory we are called to share with Him, if we remain faithful. Here below it is not the time for repose, but for toil, effort, struggle, and patience.

We know not, says St. Paul, what a weight of glory is laid up for us in return for the least suffering borne in union with Christ Jesus. "God is faithful," and in all the vicissitudes through which a soul passes, He infallibly leads her to that transformation which makes her like unto His Son.

Thus our transformation into Jesus is inwardly and gradually wrought until the day comes when the soul will appear radiant in that company of the elect who bear the mark of the Lamb, those whom the Lamb transfigures because they are His own.

IX

Passiontide

"Christ . . . loved the church and delivered himself up for it that he might sanctify it."

LOVE is the deep meaning of the mystery of the Passion. *Dilexit Ecclesiam.* And the fruit of Christ's oblation of His entire self through love, is the sanctification of the Church which here means the kingdom of those who are to form the Mystical Body of Jesus.

Doubtless, first and before all, it was out of love for His Father that Jesus willed to undergo the death of the Cross. "That the world may know that I love the Father." Here is love's triumph. Because He loves the Father, He places His Father's Will above all things.

But the love that He bears towards us likewise urges Him to accept the sufferings of the Passion, and what infinitely enhances this love is the sovereign liberty wherewith Christ offered Himself.

All is perfect in His sacrifice. Perfect too in the gift offered. Christ offered the whole of Himself; His soul and body were bruised and broken by sufferings; there is no suffering that He has not known. If we read the Gospel attentively we see that the sufferings of Jesus were ordered in such a way that no member of His Sacred Body was spared. There was no fibre of His Heart but was torn by the ingratitude of the multitude, by the faithlessness of His own disciples, and by the sufferings of His Mother. He underwent all the outrages and humiliations with which a man can be oppressed. He fulfilled to the letter the prophecy of Isaias: "Many have been astonished at Thee, so shall His visage be inglorious among men. . . . There was no sightliness that we should be desirous of Him . . . and we have thought Him as it were a leper, and as one struck by God and afflicted. . . ."

In His Agony in the Garden of Olives His innocent soul was oppressed with sadness so poignant and bitter as to be enough to cause His death. *Tristis est anima mea usque ad mortem.* A God, Infinite Power and Beatitude, was overcome by sadness, fear and heaviness. The Word Incarnate knew all the sufferings that were to fall upon Him throughout the long hours of His Passion. This vision awoke in His sensitive nature all the shrinking and repulsion that a simple creature would thereby have experienced, and, in the Divinity to which His soul was united, He saw clearly all the sins of mankind, all the outrages committed against God's holiness and infinite love.

He had taken upon Himself all these iniquities; He was, as it were, clad with them; He felt all the wrath of Divine Justice weigh upon Him. He foresaw that for many men His Blood would be shed in vain, and this sight brought the grief of His Blessed Soul to its climax. But Christ accepts all. He arises and goes forth from the garden to meet His enemies.

It is here that this series of humiliations and sufferings, which we can scarcely attempt to describe, begins for Our Lord.

Betrayed by the kiss of one of His Apostles, bound by the soldiery as a malefactor, He is led before the High Priest. There He holds His peace in the midst of the false accusations brought against Him: *Ille autem tacebat.*

He only speaks to declare that He is the Son of God: *Tu dixisti, ego sum*; and this profession is the most solemn that has ever been made to the Divinity of Christ.

Peter, the chief of the Apostles, had followed His Divine Master afar off; he had promised never to forsake Him. Poor Peter, we know how he thrice denies Jesus. For Our Lord this was without doubt one of the deepest pains of that terrible night.

The soldiers set a guard round Jesus and load Him with insults and cruelty. Not being able to bear His gentle gaze, they blindfold Him in derision; they insolently strike Him; they dare to defile with their filthy spittle that Adorable Face whereof the contemplation ravishes the Angels.

The Gospel next shows us how Jesus, from break of day, is dragged from tribunal to tribunal; how He, Eternal Wisdom, is treated by Herod as a fool and scourged by order of Pilate. And yet this cruel scourging at the hands of His pitiless executioners does not suffice for these men who do not deserve the name of men. They press a crown of thorns upon the head of their innocent Victim and make Him the butt of their mockeries.

The cowardly Roman governor imagines that the Jews' hatred will be satisfied in seeing Christ in such a pitiable state; he presents Him to the crowd. *Ecce homo!* "Behold the Man!" As at this moment we behold our Divine Master plunged into this abyss of sufferings and indignities, we may think that the Father, He too, presents Jesus to us and says: Behold my Son, the splendour of my glory—but "for the wickedness of My people have I struck Him." *Propter scelus populi mei percussi eum.*

Jesus hears the clamour of the furious populace who prefer a brigand before Him, and in return for all His benefits demand His death: *Crucifige, crucifige eum.*

The sentence of death is then pronounced, and Christ, taking His heavy Cross upon His lacerated shoulders, sets out on the way to Calvary. What sorrows are yet reserved for Him! The sight of His Mother whom He so tenderly loves, and whose immense affliction He understands as none other can, the being stripped of His garments, the piercing of His Hands and Feet, the burning thirst, the malignant sarcasm of His mortal foes. "Vah! thou that destroyest the temple of God, save thy own self, and we will believe thee." "He saved others, Himself he cannot save." Finally, the abandonment by His Father Whose holy will He has ever done: "My God, My God, why hast Thou forsaken Me!"

He has truly drunk the chalice to the dregs, He has fulfilled to the last iota, that is to say to the last detail, all that was foretold of Him. Thus, when all is accomplished, when He had exhausted to the depths every sorrow and humiliation, He can utter His *Consummatum est.* Yes, all is consummated. He has now only to give up His soul to His Father: *Et inclinato capite, tradidit spiritum.*

CHRIST'S sacrifice, begun at the moment of the Incarnation, is now achieved. From the pierced side of Jesus flow the streams of living water which are to purify and sanctify the Church. This is the perfect fruit of this perfect immolation. "For by one oblation He has perfected forever them that are sanctified."

By His sacrifice, Christ destroyed sin and restored grace to us. According to the expression of St. Paul, Christ, in letting Himself be nailed to the Cross, blotted out "the handwriting of the decree (of condemnation and death) that was against us" and reconciled us for ever to His Father. Through love, Christ made Himself surety for our sins, and we, through grace, have solidarity in His satisfaction.

THE death of Jesus is the source of our confidence, but that it may have its full effect, we ourselves must share in His Passion. Upon the Cross, Christ Jesus represented us all, but although He suffered for all, He applies the fruit of His Immolation to us on the condition that we associate ourselves with His Sacrifice.

Each year, during Holy Week, the Church lives over again with Jesus, day by day, hour by hour, all the phases of the bitter Passion of her Divine Bridegroom.

But the Passion of Jesus holds such a large place in His life, it is so much His work, He attaches such a price to it that He has moreover willed the remembrance of it to be recalled to us every day, He has instituted a sacrifice whereby the memory and fruits of His oblation on Calvary shall be perpetuated; that is the Sacrifice of the Mass: *Hoc facite in Meam Commemorationem.*

To assist at this Holy Sacrifice, or to offer it with Christ, constitutes an intimate participation in the Passion of Jesus. We may further associate ourselves with this mystery by bearing, for love of Christ, the sufferings and trials which, in the designs of His providence, He permits us to undergo.

God gives each one of us a cross to carry. We ought to accept it without reasoning, without saying: "God might have changed such or such circumstance in my life." In the generous acceptance of our cross, we shall find union with Christ. For in bearing our own cross we truly bear our share in that of Jesus.

The Word Incarnate, Head of the Church, took His share, the greater share of sorrows; but He chose to leave to His Church, His Mystical Body, a share of suffering. St. Paul demonstrates this by a profound and strange saying: "I . . . fill up those things that are wanting of the sufferings of Christ, in my flesh, for His body which is the

Church." Is there then something wanting to the sufferings whereby Christ saved us? Certainly not; they were superabundant, immense, and their merit is infinite: *Et copiosa apud eum redemptio.* But St. Augustine tells us that the whole Christ is formed by the Church united to the Head, which is Christ; the Head has suffered all that He had to suffer; it remains for the members, if they wish to be worthy of the Head, to bear in their turn their share of sorrow. We have, then, as His members to join in His sufferings. Christ has reserved for us a share in His Passion, but in doing so, He has placed by the side of the Cross, the strength necessary to carry it.

The Passion of Jesus does not however terminate the cycle of His mysteries. When Our Lord speaks of His Passion to the Apostles, He always adds: "the third day He will rise again." This is why the Church, when she solemnly commemorates the sufferings of her Bridegroom, mingles her accents of compassion with those of triumph. The liturgical ornaments of black or purple, the strippings of the altars, the "Lamentations" borrowed from Jeremias, the silence of the bells, attest the bitter desolation that oppresses the heart of the Bride during these anniversary days of the great drama. Yet she breaks forth into the triumphant accents of the

> *Pange lingua, gloriosi*
> *Lauream certaminis. . . .*

It is the same for us. Suffering is not the last word in the

Christian life. After having shared in the Saviour's Passion we shall also share in His glory. Christ will come, when our last hour strikes, to take us with Him that we may enter into His Father's Kingdom.

The day will come, sooner than we think, when death will be near. We shall lie motionless on our bed, while those around us will be silent in their utter powerlessness to help us; we shall no longer have any contact with the outer world. The soul will be alone with Christ. We shall hear Him say to us in this our supreme and decisive agony: "You did not forsake Me in my Agony, you followed Me when I went to Calvary to die for you. Behold Me now. I am near you to help you, to take you with Me. Fear not. Have confidence, it is I." *Ego sum, nolite timere!*

X

In the Footsteps of Jesus
from the Pretorium to Calvary

WHEN Christ dwelt upon earth an all-powerful virtue went out from His Divine Person, healing bodily infirmities, enlightening the mind, and quickening the soul: *Virtus de illo exibat et sanabat omnes.*

Something analogous comes to pass when we place ourselves in contact with Jesus by faith. To those who lovingly followed Him along the road to Golgotha, or were present at His immolation, Christ surely granted special graces. This virtue that went out from Him still continues to do so; and when in a spirit of faith, compassionating His sufferings and striving to imitate Him, we follow Him from the Pretorium to Calvary and take our stand at the foot of the Cross, He gives us the same graces and makes us share in the same favours.

At each "station," Our Divine Saviour presents Himself to us in His threefold character: as the Mediator Who saves us by His merits, as the perfect Model of sublime virtues, and as the efficacious Cause Who can, through His Divine Omnipotence, produce in our souls the virtues of which He gives us the example.

BEFORE making the Way of the Cross, it is well to recall St. Paul's recommendation: "Let this mind be in you which was also in Christ Jesus. . . . He humbled Himself, becoming obedient unto death, even to the death of the Cross." The more we enter into the dispositions that filled the Heart of Jesus as He passed along the Sorrowful Way—love towards His Father, charity towards men, humility, obedience, hatred of sin—the more our soul will receive graces and lights, because the Father will behold in us a more perfect image of His Son.

Jesus is Condemned to Death by Pilate

"AND Jesus stood before the governor." He stands, because, being the second Adam, He is the head of the whole race which He is about to redeem by His immolation. The first Adam merited death by his sin. Jesus, innocent but laden with the sins of the world, is to expiate them by His sacrifice. Through the clamour made by the chief priests, the Pharisees, His own nation, our sins cry out and tumultuously demand the death of the Just: *Tolle, tolle, crucifige eum.*

If Jesus stands because He is our Head and to give testimony to the truth of His doctrine and we adore thee, O Christ, and we praise thee—the Divinity of His Person and mission, He yet humbles Himself in inward self-abasement before the sentence pronounced by Pilate in whom He acknowledges an authentic power. He voluntarily accepts the sentence of condemnation in order to restore life to us.

My Divine Master, I unite myself to Your Sacred Heart in its perfect submission and utter abandonment to the Father's Will. May the virtue of Your grace produce in my soul that spirit of submission which will yield me up unreservedly and without murmuring to the Divine good pleasure and to all that it shall please You to send me at the hour when I must leave this world.

Jesus is Laden With His Cross

"THEN therefore (Pilate) delivered Him to them to be crucified. And they took Jesus, and led Him forth, bearing His own cross."

At that moment, Jesus accepted the increase of suffering that this heavy burden laid upon His bruised shoulders brought to Him. He accepted the bitter sarcasms, the malignant blasphemies which His worst enemies, apparently triumphant, were about to heap upon Him as soon as they saw Him hung upon the infamous gibbet: He accepted the three hours' agony, the being forsaken by His Father. . . . At that moment, too, Christ Jesus Who represented us all, and was going to die for us, accepted the cross for all His members, for each one of us. He then united to His own sufferings all those of His Mystical Body.

My Jesus, I accept all the crosses, all the trials, all the

adversities that the Father has destined for me. May the unction of Your grace give me strength to bear them with the submission of which You gave us the example in receiving Yours for us.

Jesus Falls the First Time Under the Cross

"HE shall be a man of sorrows, and acquainted with infirmity." This prophecy of Isaias is fulfilled to the letter. Jesus, exhausted by His sufferings of soul and body, sinks beneath the weight of the cross. He, the Almighty, falls from weakness. By this weakness He expiates our sins, repairs the revolt of our pride, and raises up a fallen world, powerless to save itself. Moreover, at that moment He merited for us the grace to humble ourselves for our sins, to acknowledge our falls, and sincerely to confess them. He merited for us the grace of fortitude to sustain our weakness.

O Christ Jesus, prostrate beneath Your cross, I adore You. "Power of God" leave me not to myself for I am but frailty. May Your power dwell in me, so that I fall not into evil.

Jesus Meets His Blessed Mother

THE DAY has come for the Blessed Virgin whereon Simeon's prophecy is to be fulfilled in her: "Thy own soul a sword shall pierce." In the same way that she was united to Jesus when offering Him in the Temple in years gone by, so now in this hour when Jesus is about to consummate His sacrifice she enters more than ever into His dispositions and shares His sufferings. She sets out towards Calvary where she knows that her Son is to be crucified. Upon the way she meets Him. What an immense sorrow to see Him in this terrible state: Her gaze meets His, and the abyss of Christ's sufferings calls upon the abyss of His Mother's compassion.

O Mother, behold your Son. By the love that we bear towards Him, obtain for us that the remembrance of His sufferings may everywhere follow us. It is in His Name that we ask this of you; to refuse it to us would be to refuse it to Him since we are His members. O Christ Jesus, behold Your Mother. For her sake grant that we may compassionate Your sorrows so that we may become like unto You.

Simon the Cyrenean Helps Jesus to Carry His Cross

"AND going out they found a man of Cyrene, named Simon, him they forced to take up His cross."

Jesus is exhausted. Although He is the Almighty, He wills that His Sacred Humanity, laden with all the sins of the world, shall feel the weight of justice and expiation. But He wants us to help Him carry His cross. Simon represents us all, and Christ asks all of us to share in His sufferings. We are His disciples only upon this condition. "If any man will come after Me, let him . . . take up his cross and follow Me."

But in His cross He has placed the unction which makes ours tolerable, for in carrying our cross, it is truly His own which we accept. He unites our sufferings to His sorrow, and by this union He confers upon them an inestimable value, the source of great merits.

My Jesus, I accept from Your Hand the particles that You detach for me from Your Cross. I accept all the disappointments, sufferings, and sorrows that You permit or that it pleases You to send me. I accept them as my share of expiation.

A Woman Wipes the Face of Jesus

TRADITION relates that a woman, touched with compassion, drew near to Jesus and offered Him a linen cloth to wipe His adorable Face. Isaias foretold of the suffering Jesus: "There is no beauty in Him, nor comeliness, and we have seen Him, and there was no sightliness, that we should be desirous of Him."

The Gospel tells us that during those terrible hours after His apprehension the soldiers had dealt Him insolent blows, and had spat in His Face; the crowning of thorns had caused the blood to trickle down His Sacred Countenance. Christ Jesus willed that we should be healed by the bruises that His Divine Face received for us. Being our Elder Brother, He restored to us, by substituting Himself for us in His Passion, the grace that makes us the children of His Father.

O Heavenly Father, in return for the bruises that Thy Son Jesus willed to suffer for us, glorify Him, exalt Him, give unto Him that splendour which He merited when His Adorable Countenance was disfigured for our salvation.

Jesus Falls the Second Time

AGAIN we see our Divine Saviour sinking under the weight of the cross. God had laid the weight of all the sins of the world upon His shoulders. They are our sins that crush Him. He beholds them in all their multitude and in their every detail. He accepts them as if they were His own to the extent that He no longer appears, according to St. Paul's words, anything but a living sin: *Eum pro nobis peccatum fecit.* Being the Eternal Word, Jesus is all-powerful but He chooses to feel all the weakness of a burdened humanity. This wholly voluntary weakness honours the justice of His Heavenly Father, and merits strength for us.

O Jesus, become weak for love of me, crushed beneath the weight of my sins, give me the strength that is in You so that You alone may be glorified by my deeds.

Jesus Speaks to the Women of Jerusalem

"AND there followed Him a great multitude of people and of women, who bewailed and lamented Him. But Jesus, turning to them said: Daughters of Jerusalem, weep not over Me; but weep for yourselves and for your children. For behold the days shall come, wherein they will say: Blessed are the barren. . . . For if in the green wood they do these things, what shall be done in the dry?"

Jesus knows the ineffable exigencies of His Father's justice and holiness. He reminds the daughters of Jerusalem that this justice and holiness are adorable perfections of the Divine Being. Let us implore mercy against the dreadful day when Jesus will come, no longer as a Victim bowed down beneath the weight of our sins but as the Sovereign Judge to Whom the Father has given all power.

O Jesus, True Vine, grant that I may remain united to You by grace and good works so that I may bear fruit worthy of You. Grant that I may not become, through my sins, a dead branch good for nothing but to be gathered up and cast into the fire.

Jesus Falls For the Third Time

"THE LORD was pleased to bruise Him in infirmity," said Isaias, speaking of Christ during His Passion. Jesus is crushed beneath the weight of Divine Justice. None other has borne the weight of it in all its fulness; not even the damned. But the Sacred Humanity of Jesus, united to this Divine Justice by immediate contact, underwent all its power and rigour. As the Victim Who delivered Himself out of love to all its action, He falls prostrate, crushed and broken beneath its weight.

O my Jesus, teach me to detest sin which obliges justice to require of You such expiation. Grant me to unite all my sufferings to Yours so that by them my sins may be blotted out and I may make satisfaction even here below.

Jesus is Stripped of His Garments

"THEY parted My garments amongst them; and upon My vesture they cast lots." This is the prophecy of the Psalmist. Jesus is stripped of everything and placed in the nakedness of utter poverty. He does not even dispose of His garments for as soon as He is raised upon the cross, the soldiers divide them among themselves and cast lots for His coat.

Nothing is so glorious to God or so useful to our souls as to unite the offering of ourselves, absolutely and without condition, to the offering which Jesus made at the moment when He gave Himself up to the executioners to be stripped of His raiment and fastened to the cross "that through His poverty we might be rich."

O my Jesus, accept the offering that I make to You of my whole being. Join it to that which You made to Your Heavenly Father at the moment of reaching Calvary. Strip me of all attachment to created things and to myself.

Jesus is Nailed to the Cross

"THEY crucified Him, and with Him two others, one on each side, and Jesus in the midst." Jesus delivers Himself up to His executioners, "dumb as a lamb before his shearers."

Jesus unceasingly gazes in to the face of His Father and with incommensurable love He yields up His body to repair the insults offered to the Eternal Majesty.

He delivers Himself likewise for us. Each one can repeat in all truth the burning words of St. Paul: "He loved me, and delivered Himself up for me." What a revelation of the love of Jesus for us! And this love is likewise the love of the Father and the Holy Spirit, for these Three are but One.

O Jesus, Who "in obeying the will of the Father and through the co-operation of the Holy Ghost, did by Your death give life to the world, deliver me by Your most sacred Body and Blood from all my iniquities and from all evils. . . ."†

Jesus Dies Upon the Cross

"AND Jesus crying with a loud voice said: Father, into Thy hands I commend My spirit. And saying this, He gave up the ghost." After three hours of indescribable sufferings, Jesus dies. The only oblation worthy of God, the one sacrifice that redeems the world and sanctifies souls, is consummated.

Christ Jesus had promised that when He should be lifted up from the earth, He would draw all things to

† Ordinary of the Mass.

Himself. Let us implore Him to draw us to His Sacred
Heart by the virtue of His death upon the Cross; to grant
that we may die to our self-love and self-will, the sources
of so many infidelities and sins, and that we may live only
for Him Who died for us.

O Father, glorify Thy Son hanging upon the gibbet.
Since He humbled Himself even to the death of the Cross,
exalt Him. May the name that Thou hast given Him be
glorified, may every knee bow before Him and every
tongue confess that Thy Son Jesus lives henceforward in
Thy eternal glory!

The Body of Jesus is Taken Down
From the Cross and Given to His Mother

THE mangled body of Jesus is restored to Mary. We cannot imagine the grief of the Blessed Virgin at this
moment. Never did mother love her child as Mary loved
Jesus. The Holy Spirit had fashioned within her a mother's
heart to love a God-Man. Never did human heart beat
with more tenderness for the Word Incarnate than did the
heart of Mary, for she was full of grace and her love met
with no obstacle to its expansion.

Then she owed all to Jesus; her Immaculate Concep-
tion, the privileges which made of her a unique creature
had been given to her in prevision of the Death of her
Son. What unutterable sorrow was hers when she
received the bloodstained Body of Jesus within her arms!

O Mother, fount of love, make me understand the strength of your love so that I may share your grief. Make my heart glow with love for Christ, my God, that I may think only of pleasing Him.

Jesus is Laid in the Sepulchre

JOSEPH of Arimathea having taken the Body of Jesus down from the cross, "wrapped Him in fine linen, and laid Him in a sepulchre that was hewed in stone, wherein never yet any man had been laid."

St. Paul tells us that "we are buried together with Him by baptism." The sacramental virtue of our baptism forever endures. In uniting ourselves by faith and love to Christ laid in the tomb, we renew the grace of dying to sin in order to live only for God.

Lord Jesus, may I bury in Your tomb all my sins, my failings, my infidelities. By the virtue of Your Death and Burial, give me grace to renounce more and more all that separates me from You. By the virtue of Your Resurrection, grant that, like You, I may no longer live save for the glory of Your Father.

XI

Paschal Time

Si Consurrexistis cum Christo

IN HER LITANIES, the Church applies certain qualify-
ing titles to some of the mysteries of Jesus. She says of
His Resurrection that it is "holy," *Per sanctam resurrectionem
tuam.*

Why is the Resurrection, in preference to all the other
mysteries of Jesus, called "holy" by the Church?

Because it is in this mystery that Christ particularly fulfils the conditions of holiness; in His Resurrection, Christ
is above all the Example of holiness.

Holiness can be divided for us into two elements—separation from all sin, detachment from every creature, and
the belonging totally and steadfastly to God.

In Christ's Resurrection these two characters are found
in a degree unmanifested until His coming forth from the
tomb. Although the Word Incarnate had been, during His
entire existence, the "Holy One" like to none other, it is
with effulgent brightness that He especially reveals Himself to us under this aspect in His Resurrection and it is
therefore that the Church sings: *Per sanctam resurrectionem
tuam.*

His Risen Body is henceforward immortal. Christ "died once," but, says St. Paul, "Christ rising again from the dead, dieth now no more, death shall no more have dominion over Him": *Mors illi ultra non dominabitur.* The body of the Risen Jesus is no longer subject to death nor to the conditions of time; it is impassible, spiritual, living in a supreme independence.

In Christ is here represented the first element of holiness—separation from all that is dead, from all that is earthly. On the day of His Resurrection, Christ Jesus leaves in the tomb the linen cloths which are the symbol of our infirmities, our weaknesses and imperfections. He comes forth free and triumphant from the sepulchre. His liberty is entire, He is animated with intense, perfect life with which all the fibres of His being vibrate. In Him, all that is mortal is absorbed by Life.

Doubtless we shall see the Risen Jesus still touching earth. Out of love for His disciples and condescension for the weakness of their faith, He vouchsafes to appear to them, to converse with them, to share their repasts, but His life is before all things heavenly: *Vivit Deo.*

This is the second element of holiness—the adhering, the belonging, the consecration to God. We shall only know in Heaven with what plenitude Jesus lived for His Father during those blessed days; it was certainly with a perfection that ravished the angels. Now that His Sacred Humanity is set free from all the necessities, from all the infirmities of our earthly condition, it yields itself more

utterly than ever before to the glory of the Father. The life
of the Risen Jesus becomes an infinite source of glory for
His Father; all within Him is light, strength, beauty, life;
all within Him sings an uninterrupted canticle of praise.

IT is from our Baptism that we share in this grace of the
Resurrection. St. Paul affirms this: "We are buried
together with Him by Baptism unto death; that as Christ
is risen from the dead by the power of the Father, so we
also may walk in newness of life."
The holy water into which we are plunged at baptism is,
according to the Apostle, the figure of the sepulchre.
Upon coming forth from it the soul is purified from all
sin, from all stain, set free from all spiritual death, and
clad with grace, the principle of divine life. In the early
Church, baptism was administered only on the Paschal
night, and at Pentecost which closes the Paschal season.
We shall scarcely understand anything of the liturgy of
Easter week if we do not keep before our eyes the thought
of baptism which was then solemnly conferred upon the
catechumens.

WE are therefore risen with Christ, through Christ, for
He infinitely longs to communicate His glorious life to us.
And what is necessary in order to respond to this Divine
longing and become like unto the Risen Jesus? It is that
we should live in the spirit of our baptism. Renouncing all
that sin has vitiated in our lives, we should die more and

more to "the old man" and all within us should be domi-
nated and governed by grace. All holiness for us lies in
this—to keep away from all sin, all occasion of sin, and be
detached from all that is earthly so as to live in God, unto
God, with the greatest plenitude and steadfastness possible.

This work begun at baptism continues during our
whole earthly existence. Christ, it is true, dies but once,
but we must die daily, for we have the roots of sin remain-
ing in us and the old enemy labours unceasingly to make
them spring up. To destroy these roots in us, to keep our
hearts free, with a spiritual freedom, such is the first element of our holiness which Christ shows us realised in
Him by this supreme and admirable independence
wherein His Risen Humanity lives.

This life unto God comprises an infinity of degrees. To
begin with it supposes one to be totally separated from all
mortal sin; between mortal sin and the divine life there is
absolute incompatibility. Next there is separation from
venial sin, from all natural springs of action, and detachment from all that is created. The more complete this separation is the more we are spiritually free, and the more
also the divine life develops and expands within us. In the
same measure that the soul is freed from what is earthly
she opens to what is divine, she savours heavenly things,
she lives for God.

In this happy state, the soul is not only free from sin,
but she no longer acts save under the inspiration of grace

and from a supernatural motive. And when this supernatural motive extends to all her actions, when by a movement of habitual and steadfast love she refers all to God, to the glory of Christ and that of His Father, then there is within her the plentitude of life. That is holiness.

We cannot attain to it in a day. Holiness ingrafted in us by baptism, is only developed little by little, by successive stages. Let us try to act in such a way that each Easter, each day of this blessed season which extends from the Resurrection to Pentecost, may produce within us a more complete death to sin and to the creature, and a more vigorous and abundant increase of the life of Christ.

Christ must reign in our hearts, and all within us must be subject to Him. Since the day of His triumph, He gloriously lives and reigns in God in the bosom of the Father: *Vivit et regnat Deus.* Christ only lives where He reigns, and He lives in us in the same degree as He reigns in our soul.

IN pointing out the double aspect of the mystery of holiness that the Resurrection of Jesus ought to produce within our hearts we have not yet exhausted the riches of Paschal grace.

God is so magnificent in what He does for His Christ that He wills the mystery of His Son's Resurrection to extend not only to our souls but also to our bodies. We too shall rise again. That is a dogma of faith. We shall rise corporally like Christ, with Christ. Could it be otherwise?

If Christ is risen—and He is risen in His human nature—it is necessary that we, His members, should share in the same glory. For it is not only in our soul, it is likewise in our body, in our whole being that we are members of Christ. The most intimate union binds us to Him. If then He is risen glorious, the faithful who by grace make part of His Mystical Body will be united to Him even in His Resurrection.

Hear what St. Paul says on this subject: "Christ is risen from the dead, the first-fruits of them that sleep." He represents the first-fruits of a harvest; after Him the rest of the harvest is to follow. "By a man came death, and by a man the resurrection of the dead. And as in Adam all die, so also in Christ all shall be made alive." God, he says more energetically still, "has raised us up together . . . through Jesus Christ": *Conresuscitavit nos . . . in Christo Jesu.* As grace is the principle of our glory, those who are, by grace, already saved in hope, are already also, in principle, risen in Christ. This is our faith and our hope.

BUT now "our life is hidden with Christ in God." During our earthly life grace does not produce those effects of light and splendour which will have their fruition in glory. Our inner life here below is known only to God; it is hidden from the eyes of men. Moreover, if we try to reproduce in our souls, by our spiritual liberty, the characteristics of the Risen Life of Jesus it is a labour which is still wrought in a flesh wounded by sin, subject to the

88

infirmities of time. We can only attain this holy liberty at the cost of a struggle incessantly renewed and faithfully sustained. We too must suffer in order to enter into glory, as Christ said of Himself to the disciples of Emmaus on the very day of His Resurrection: *Nonne haec oportuit pati Christum et ita intrare in gloriam suam?* "We are the sons of God," says the Apostle, "and if sons, heirs also; heirs indeed of God, and joint heirs with Christ; yet so if we suffer with Him, that we may be also glorified with Him."

May these thoughts of Heaven sustain us during the days we have yet to pass here below. Yes, the time will come when there shall be no more mourning, nor crying, nor sorrow; God Himself will wipe away the tears of His servants become the co-heirs with His Son; He will make them sit down at the eternal feast which He has prepared to celebrate the triumph of Jesus and of those whose Elder Brother Jesus is.

XII

The Feast of the Ascension

". . .And Now, Father, Glorify Thy Son"

O F ALL the Feasts of Our Lord, I venture to say that, in a certain sense, the Ascension is the greatest because it is the supreme glorification of Christ Jesus. Holy Church calls the Ascension "admirable" and "glorious," and throughout the Divine Office of this Feast she makes us hymn the magnificence of this mystery.

Our Divine Saviour had asked of His Father to be glorified with that glory which He had, in His Divinity, in the eternal splendours of Heaven: *Clarifica Me, Tu, Pater . . . claritate quam habui priusquam mundus esset apud te.* The triumph of the Resurrection was the dawn of this personal glorification of Jesus. The admirable Ascension places it in full noontide. It is the divine glorification of Christ's Humanity above the highest heavens.

THE Mystery of Jesus Christ's Ascension is represented to us in a manner comfortable to our nature; we contemplate the Sacred Humanity rising from the earth and ascending visibly towards the heavens.

For the last time Jesus assembles His disciples and leads

them towards Bethany on the Mount of Olives. He gives them anew the mission of preaching to all the world, while promising to be ever with them by His grace and the action of His Spirit.[†] Then, having blessed them, He rises by His own Divine power above the clouds and disappears from their gaze.

It was at the foot at the Mount of Olives that His Passion began, and now Jesus, Eternal Wisdom, chooses the summit of the same mountain that had witnessed His sorrowful agony from whence to ascend to heaven.

THIS material Ascension, real and wonderful though it be, is at the same time the symbol of an ascension of which the Apostles themselves did not see the term, an ascension yet more wonderful and incomprehensible for us. Our Saviour rises *super omnes cælos*, "above all the heavens," passing all the angelic choirs, staying only at the right hand of God: *Assumptus est in cælum, et sedet a dextris Dei.*

Jesus is God and Man. As God, He fills heaven and earth with His Divine Presence; it is therefore as Man that He arose to the right hand of the Father. But the Humanity in Jesus is united to the Person of the Word; it is the Humanity of a God and in this quality it enjoys the right of Divine glory in the eternal splendours.

† He dwells with us also by the Real Presence in the Sacrament of the Eucharist.

We have seen that from the dawn of His Resurrection Jesus entered into the possession of this resplendent glory; His Humanity was henceforth glorious and impassible. But it still remained here below in this world where death reigns. To attain the summit, the full expansion of this glory, the Risen Jesus had need of an abode corresponding fittingly to His new condition; He needed the heights of heaven whence His glory and might radiate in their fulness upon the whole company of the elect.

AND as for ourselves shall we not penetrate into the heavens? Are we to remain shut out from this sojourn of glory and beatitude? Have we no part in the Ascension of Jesus? Certainly we have, but, as we know, it is through Christ and in Christ that we enter into heaven.

That glorious train, the souls of the just, who escorted Jesus in His triumphal ascent into heaven were but the first-fruits of innumerable harvests. Unceasingly souls are ascending into heaven until that day when the Kingdom of Jesus shall have attained the measure of its fulness.

St. Leo says: "Christ's Ascension is therefore also our own; upon the glory of the Head rests the hope of the body. On this holy day we have received not only the assurance of entering into possession of eternal glory, but we have already entered into the heights of heaven with Christ Jesus."[†] The wiles of the old enemy tore us away

† S. Leo. Sermo 1. *De Ascensione Domini.*

from the first sojourn of delight, the earthly paradise; the Son of God in incorporating us with Himself placed us at the right hand of His Father.

Upon earth we are but as strangers and pilgrims seeking our country; as members of the city of saints and the household of God we may already dwell in Heaven by faith and hope.

By Communion, we are united to Jesus; in coming to us Our Lord grants us to share, in hope, that glory of which He enjoys the reality. He gives us the very pledge of it: *Et futurae gloriae nobis pignus datur.*†

THERE are two dispositions which especially spring from the contemplation of this mystery: they are joy and confidence.

Our Lord Himself said to His Apostles before leaving them: "If you loved Me, you would indeed be glad, because I go to the Father." Christ repeats these words to us. If we love Him we shall rejoice in His glorification and exaltation to the highest heaven. Bliss, such as is incomprehensible to us, envelops and penetrates Him forever in the bosom of the Divinity.

How can we fail to rejoice that justice is rendered in all fulness to Jesus by His Father?

SEE how the Church invites us in her Liturgy to celebrate

† Antiphon for the Feast of Corpus Christi: *O Sacrum Convivium.*

with gladness the exaltation of her Bridegroom, our God and our Redeemer.

Sometimes she urges all nations to let the fulness of their joy burst forth: "O clap your hands all ye nations; shout unto God with the voice of joy. God is ascended with jubilee, and the Lord with the sound of the trumpet. Sing praises to our God, sing ye: sing praises to our King, sing ye! Exalt the King of kings, and sing a hymn to God."

At other times the Church calls upon the angelic powers: "Lift up your gates, O ye princes, and the King of Glory shall enter in. . . . It is the Lord strong and mighty . . . it is the Lord of hosts, He is the King of glory": *Ipse est Rex gloriae!*

Again, in language full of poetry borrowed from the Psalmist, she addresses Jesus Himself: "Be Thou exalted, O Lord, in Thy own strength, we will sing and praise Thy power. . . . For Thy magnificence is elevated above the heavens. Thou hast put on praise and beauty: and art clothed with light as with a garment; Who makest the clouds Thy chariot: Who walkest upon the wings of the winds."

With this deep joy we ought to combine unshaken confidence. This confidence especially finds its support in Christ's almighty power of mediation with His Father, not only as an invincible King entering into His triumph, but as a supreme High Priest interceding for us after having offered to His Father an oblation of infinite value. Now it is on the day of the Ascension that Jesus began, in a special manner, this unique mediation. This mediation is eternal as His Priesthood is eternal.

St. Paul recalls how in the temple of Jerusalem there was a tabernacle called the Holy; the priests entered there at all times for the service of worship; beyond the veil was a second tabernacle called the Holy of Holies, where the altar of incense and the ark of the Covenant stood.

This "Holy of Holies" was the most august place upon earth. It was the centre towards which the worship and desire of Israel converged, towards which the hands of the entire Jewish people were raised, for it was there God made His special dwelling. There He received homage and heard the prayers of Israel; there He entered, so to speak, into contact with His people.

But this contact was only established by the intermediary of the high priest. So terrible indeed was the majesty of this tabernacle that only the high priest of the Jews might enter there; the entry was forbidden to any other under pain of death. The high priest entered the Holy of Holies clad in pontifical vestments, wearing upon his breast the mysterious "rational" composed of twelve precious stones on which were engraved the names of the twelve tribes of Israel; it was only in this symbolical manner that the people had access to the Holy of Holies. Moreover, the high priest himself might only cross the threshold of this holy tabernacle once a year; and first he had to immolate outside two victims—one for his own sins, the other for the sins of the people.

Christ, says St. Paul, is the supreme High Priest, "a High Priest, holy, innocent, undefiled, separated from sinners, and made higher than the heavens." He enters into a tabernacle not made by the hand of man, but into the "heaven of heavens," in the sanctuary of the Divinity. He enters therein bearing the blood of the victim, His own Precious Blood of infinite value, shed "outside," that is to say upon the earth, and shed not for the sins of the people of Israel alone, but for the sins of all mankind. He enters through the veil, that is to say through the Sacred Humanity. It is through this veil that the way to heaven is henceforward open to us. Finally, He does not only enter there once a year, but once forever.

But—and it is above all in this that the reality transcends the figure—Christ does not enter there alone. Our High Priest takes us with Him, not in a symbolical manner but in reality, for we are His members.

WHEN we communicate during these holy days let our souls give themselves up to these thoughts of joy and confidence.

In uniting ourselves with Jesus Christ we incorporate ourselves with Him. He is in us and we are in Him. We stand in presence of the Father. Undoubtedly we do not behold Him, but, by faith, we know ourselves to be with Jesus in the bosom of the Father, in the sanctuary of the Divinity. This is for us the grace of the Ascension, namely, to share, by faith, in the ineffable intimacy that Christ Jesus has in Heaven with His Father.

XIII

Pentecost

The Mission of the Holy Spirit

"I F YOU loved Me," said Christ Jesus to His Apostles, "you would indeed be glad because I go to the Father."

But Our Lord did not only tell them that they ought to rejoice in His Ascension; He added that His Ascension would profit them. "I tell you truth; it is expedient to you that I go: for if I go not, the Paraclete will not come to you; but if I go, I will send Him to you."

Might they not have answered Him: "O Divine Master, say not so. We need none other save You; You are sufficient for us. To whom shall we go? With You have we not every grace? Abide then with us." *Mane nobiscum.*

But the Divine Master's words are formal: "It is expedient to you that I go, for if I go not, the Paraclete will not come to you."

This is the mystery that we are about to contemplate as far as is possible for us; for here all is supernatural, and faith alone can be our guide.

IN His Divine Nature, Jesus is, with the Father, the principle whence the Holy Spirit proceeds. The gift of the

Holy Spirit to the Church and to souls is a priceless gift since the Spirit is Divine Love in person. But this gift, like every grace, was merited for us by Jesus. It is the fruit of His Passion. He purchased it by the sufferings He endured in His Sacred Humanity. Was it not therefore just that this grace should not be given to the world until that Humanity, whereby it had been merited, had been glorified? It was not until the day of the Ascension that the Sacred Humanity entered definitively into possession of the glory to which it is doubly entitled as being united to the Son of God and as being a Victim offered to the Father thereby to merit every grace for souls. Seated at the right hand of the Father in the glory of Heaven, the Humanity of the Incarnate Word was to be thus associated with the "sending" of the Holy Spirit by the Father and the Son.

Moreover faith was to be the source, as it were, of the coming of the Holy Spirit in us. As long as Christ Jesus lived upon earth the faith of the disciples was imperfect. It could only unfold in its fulness when the Ascension had taken the human presence of their Divine Master from their sight.

LET us now contemplate for a few moments the Divine workings of the Holy Spirit in the souls of the Apostles on the day of Pentecost.

He fills them with *truth*. We might say: Had not Christ Jesus done this? Certainly He had. He had Himself declared: "I am the Truth." He came into the world to bear testimony to the truth, and we know also from Himself that He wholly accomplished His mission: *Opus consummavi.*

But now that He has left His Apostles, it is the Holy Spirit who is about to become their interior Master. The Apostles had no need to trouble as to what they should reply when the Jews delivered them up before the tribunals and forbade them to preach the name of Jesus. It was the Holy Spirit Who would inspire their replies. And thus they should bear witness to Jesus.

And as it is by the tongue, the organ of speech, that testimony is rendered and whereby the preaching of the name of Jesus was to go forth to the uttermosts parts of the earth, this Spirit, on the day of Pentecost, descends visibly upon the Apostles in the form of tongues.

AND these are tongues of fire, for the Holy Spirit comes to fill the hearts of the Apostles with *love.* He is personal Love in the Life of God. He is, as it were, the breath, the aspiration of the infinite love whence we drew life. It is related in Genesis that "the Lord God formed man of the slime of the earth, and breathed into his face the breath of life." This vital breath was the symbol of the Spirit to Whom we owe the supernatural life. On the day of Pentecost, the Divine Spirit brought such an abundance of life to the whole Church that to signify it "there came a sound from heaven, as of a mighty wind coming, and it filled the whole house where they were sitting."

THIS love, ardent as a flame, powerful as a tempestuous wind, is necessary to the Apostles in order that they may be enabled to meet the dangers foretold by Christ when they shall have to preach His Name: the Holy Spirit fills them with *fortitude*.

What is it that makes them speak with such courage, they who, on the night of the Passion, forsook Jesus; they who, during the days that followed the Resurrection, remained hidden with doors fast shut "for fear of the Jews"? It is the Spirit of Truth, the Spirit of Love, the Spirit of Fortitude.

WHENCE too came their joy in suffering and humiliations? From the Holy Spirit, for He is not only the Spirit of Fortitude, He is also the Spirit of *Consolation*. "I will ask the Father," says Jesus, "and He shall give you another Paraclete."

Is not Christ Jesus Himself a Consoler? Did He not say: "Come to Me, all ye that labour and are burdened, and I will refresh you?"

Yes, but this Divine Consoler was to disappear from the earthly eyes of the disciples; that is why He asked His Father to send them *another* Consoler, equal to Himself, God like Himself,

Because He is the Spirit of Truth, this Consoler assuages the needs of our intelligence; because He is the Spirit of Love, He satisfies the desires of our heart; because He is the Spirit of Strength, He sustains us in our toils, trials and tears. The Holy Ghost is pre-eminently the Consoler.

> *Consolator optime,*
> *Dulcis hospes animae,*
> *Dulce refrigerium.*

Oh, come and dwell in us, Father of the poor, Giver of heavenly gifts, Thou best Consoler, sweet Guest, and Refreshment full of sweetness for the soul!

THE Holy Spirit came for us. Those assembled in the Cenacle represented the whole Church. The Spirit comes that He may abide with her forever.

The Holy Ghost descended visibly upon the Apostles at Pentecost. From that day forward the Holy Church has been spreading over all the earth. She is the Kingdom of Jesus, and it is the Holy Spirit Who, with the Father and the Son, governs His Kingdom. He completes in souls the work of sanctification begun by the Redemption. He is, in the Church, what the soul is in the body: the Spirit that animates and quickens it, the Spirit that safeguards unity, whilst His action produces manifold effects; He brings her all her vigour and beauty.

HISTORICALLY and as a visible mission, Pentecost is doubtless ended, but the inward action of the Spirit is unceasing. Its virtue endures forever, its grace remains. The Holy Spirit's mission in souls is henceforth invisible, but it is none the less fruitful.

The Church prays as if Pentecost were to be renewed for us; she repeats the antiphon *Rex gloriæ* each day during the octave of the Ascension. Then on the day of the solemnity of Pentecost, she multiplies her praises to the Holy Spirit in language full of magnificence and poetry: "Come, Holy Spirit, fill the hearts of Thy faithful and kindle in them the fire of Thy love. Come and from the height of heaven send down on us a ray of Thy light! O most blessed Light, fill our inmost hearts with Thy radiance! Fount of Living Water, Fire of Love, spiritual Unction, come! Shed Thy light in our minds, pour forth Thy charity into our hearts, strengthen our weakness with Thy unfailing strength!"

We may perhaps say: Have we not already received the Holy Spirit at Baptism, and yet more specially in the Sacrament of Confirmation?

Assuredly we have, but we can always receive Him more abundantly. We can always receive from Him clearer light and greater strength. He can always cause deeper wellsprings of consolation to rise up in our souls and enkindle an intenser love within our hearts.

And this fruitful working of the Spirit within us can be renewed not only during the holy days of Pentecost but moreover each time that we receive a Sacrament. The Holy Ghost comes to dwell within us; He remains in order to sanctify us, to guide all our supernatural activity. He enriches us, bestows upon us His gifts of wisdom and understanding, of counsel and fortitude, of knowledge, piety, and fear of the Lord, which make us act as children of God: *Quicumque Spiritu Dei aguntur in sunt filii Dei.*

This Divine Guest, full of loving kindness, makes His abode in our hearts that He may help and strengthen us. He will only leave us if we have the misfortune to drive Him from our souls by mortal sin. To drive out this Spirit of Love by preferring the creature to Him in an absolute manner is what St. Paul calls "to quench the Spirit." Moreover, let us follow the Apostle's counsel and not "grieve" the Spirit; do not let us resist His inspirations by any fully deliberate fault, however slight, by wilfully replying "no" to the good He suggests to us.

His action is extremely delicate, and when the soul resists Him deliberately and frequently, she forces Him little by little to be silent. Then she comes to a standstill in the path of holiness and even incurs great risk of leaving the way of salvation. What can such a soul do without a master to guide her, without light to enlighten her, without strength to sustain her, without joy to transport her?

Let us be faithful to this Spirit Who comes, with the Father and the Son, to take up His abode within us. "Know ye not," says St. Paul again, "that you are the temple of God, and that the Spirit of God dwelleth in you?" Each increase of grace is like a new reception of this Divine Guest, a new taking possession of our souls by Him, a new embrace of love.

XIV

Corpus Christi

In Mei Memoriam

IN EACH of Christ's mysteries there is enough shadow to render our faith meritorious and there is also enough light to help our faith. In all we see manifested the ineffable union of the Divinity with the Humanity.

But there is one mystery in which the Divinity and Humanity far from being revealed both disappear from our senses. This is the mystery of the Eucharist.

Before the Consecration there is upon the altar a little bread, a little wine. And after the Consecration there is, for the senses, still bread and wine. Faith alone penetrates beneath these veils, even to the divine reality therein totally hidden. Without faith we shall never see anything but bread and wine; we do not see God, He does not here reveal Himself as in the Gospel. We do not even see His Manhood.

When during His earthly life, Christ declared that He was the Son of God, He gave proof that He was so. It was indeed clear that He was a man, but a Man Whose doctrine could come only from God; a Man Who wrought wonders that only God could work. Faith was necessary, but the miracles of Jesus and the sublimity of His teaching helped the faith of the Jews, the simple as well as the wise.

In the Eucharist there is room only for pure faith, founded solely upon the words of Jesus: "This is My Body, this is My Blood."The Eucharist is above all a mystery of faith, *Mysterium fidei*.

WHEN our Divine Saviour instituted this mystery in view of perpetuating the fruits of His Sacrifice, He said to His Apostles: *Hoc facite in Meam commemorationem*. "Do this for a commemoration of Me." Thus besides the primary object of renewing His immolation and making us participate in it by Communion, Christ desired to make of it, in addition, a memorial.

The Eucharist is a memorial and brings the remembrance of Christ to our hearts first of all as being a sacrifice.

Certainly, as we know, there is only one total and perfect sacrifice that has paid off and expiated all, that has merited everything and from which every grace flows: this is the Sacrifice of Calvary; there is none other.

But in order that the merits of this Sacrifice may be applied to every soul of every time, Christ willed that it should be renewed upon the altar. The altar is another Calvary where the immolation on the Cross is commemorated, represented, and reproduced. Thus wherever a priest is to be found to consecrate the bread and wine, the remembrance of the Passion is kept. That which is offered and given upon the altar is the Body which was broken for us, the Blood which was shed for our salvation. It is the same High Priest, Christ Jesus, Who still offers them through the ministry of His Priests. Hence we cannot fail to think of the Passion when we assist at the Sacrifice of the Mass where all is identical, except the manner in which the oblation is accomplished.

But although the Eucharist recalls (in a direct manner and in the first place) the Passion of Jesus, it does not exclude the remembrance of the glorious mysteries linked so closely to the Passion of which they are, in a sense, the crown.

Since it is Christ's Body and Blood that we receive, the Eucharist supposes the Incarnation and the mysteries founded upon it or flowing from it. Christ is upon the altar with the Divine life which never ceases, with His mortal life of which the historical form has doubtless ceased, but of which the substance and merits remain with the glorious life which shall have no end.

All this is really contained in the Sacred Host and given in Communion to our soul. In communicating Himself to us, Christ gives Himself in the substantial totality of His works and mysteries, as in the oneness of His Person.

The Eucharist is, as it were, the synthesis of the marvels of the love of the Incarnate Word towards us.

IF we now consider the Eucharist as a Sacrament, we shall discover in it wonderful properties which only a God could invent.

According to Our Lord's own words one of the most characteristic figures of the Eucharist was the manna. With special insistence, our Divine Saviour compared this food, which came down from Heaven to nourish the Hebrews in the desert, with the Eucharistic Bread which He was about to give to the world. "Your fathers did eat manna in the desert and are dead. This is the Bread which cometh down from Heaven; that if any man eat of it, he may not die. I am the Living Bread which came down from Heaven; if any man eat of this Bread, he shall live for ever"—for it places in our very bodies the germ of the Resurrection. "And the Bread that I will give is My Flesh for the life of the world. . . ."

It was in the midst of a repast, under the form of food, that Our Lord chose to institute the Eucharist.

Nothing is so joyous as a feast. Holy Communion is the feast of the soul, that is to say a source of deepest joys. It is one of the effects of the Eucharist when received with devotion to fill the soul with supernatural sweetness, rendering it prompt in God's service.

We must not forget, however, that this joy is above all spiritual. The Eucharist being preeminently the "mystery of faith," it may happen that God permits that this altogether inward joy should not react upon the sensible part of our being. It may happen that even very fervent souls remain in a state of great dryness after having received the Bread of Life. They must not be discouraged at this. If they have brought all the necessary dispositions for receiving Christ and still suffer from their powerlessness, they may be reassured and remain in peace. Christ, ever living, acts silently but supremely in the innermost depths of the soul in order to transform it into Himself. That is the most precious effect of the Heavenly Food: "He that eateth My Flesh and drinketh My Blood, abideth in Me, and I in him."

OF all the properties that Holy Scriptures attributes to the manna, there is one particularly remarkable. The manna was a food which accommodated itself to the taste and wishes of the one who partook of it, being "turned to what every man liked."

In the Heavenly Bread, the Eucharist, we can also find the savour of all Christ's mysteries and the virtue of all His states.

When, therefore, we receive Christ at the Holy Table we may contemplate Him and converse with Him in any of His mysteries. Although He is now in His glorious state, we find in Him the One Who has lived for us and merited for us the grace that these mysteries contain. Dwelling in us, Christ communicates this grace to us in order to effect little by little that transformation of our life into Him which is the effect proper to the Sacrament.

The Eucharist Sacrifice gives us the Sacrament. It is only by being united to the victim that we perfectly participate in the Sacrifice.

By Communion we perfectly enter into the intentions

of Jesus, we fully respond to what were the desires of His Heart on the day when He instituted the Eucharist: "Take ye and eat."

WHAT a sanctuary is the soul that has just received Holy Communion! The Eucharist first of all gives us Christ's Body and Blood. It gives us the Divinity of the Word indissolubly united to the Human Nature; through the Word, our soul is united to the Father and the Spirit in the indivisibility of Their uncreated nature. The Trinity dwells within us; our soul becomes the heaven whence are wrought the mysterious operations of the Divine Life. To the Father we can offer the Son of His dilection in Whom He ever finds His delight; we can offer this delight to Jesus so that the ineffable joys that He experienced at the moment of His Incarnation may be renewed within His blessed Soul; we can pray the Holy Spirit to be the bond of love uniting us to the Father and the Son. . . .

Faith alone can comprehend these marvels and fathom these abysses: *Mysterium fidei.*

XV

The Feast of the Sacred Heart

WHEN we consider the mysteries of Jesus, it is love which we see especially shine out. Love brought about the Incarnation. Love caused Christ to be born in weak and passible flesh, it inspired the obscurity of the hidden life and nourished the zeal of the public life. If Jesus delivers Himself up to death for us, it is because He yields to the excess of a measureless love; if He rises again it is for our justification; if He ascends into Heaven it is to prepare a place for us in this abode of blessedness; He sends the Paraclete so as not to leave us orphans; He institutes the Blessed Sacrament as a memorial of His love.

Nothing urges us to love like knowing and feeling ourselves to be loved. "Every time that we think of Jesus Christ," says St. Teresa, "let us remember the love with which He has heaped His benefits upon us. . . . Love calls forth love."

THERE is one feast which by its object brings to mind, in a general manner, the love that the Word Incarnate has shown to us: it is the Feast of the Sacred Heart.

NOW that we have passed in review the chief mysteries of

our Divine Lord, I will say a few words about the devotion to the Sacred Heart, its object and its practice. We shall grasp once more this important truth that for us all is summed up in the practical knowledge of Christ Jesus.

DEVOTION to the Sacred Heart is to be understood, speaking generally, as devotion to the Person of Jesus Himself, manifesting His love for us and showing us His Heart as a symbol of this love. The immediate, special object of this devotion is the Heart of Jesus, the Heart which beats for us in the bosom of the God-Man; but we do not honour it apart from the Human Nature of Jesus nor from the Person of the Eternal Word united to this Human Nature in the Incarnation.

RELATIVELY modern under the form that it actually bears, devotion to the Sacred Heart has its dogmatic roots in the deposit of faith. It was contained in germ in the words of St. John: "The Word was made Flesh, and dwelt among us. . . . Having loved His own . . . He loved them unto the end."

What is the Incarnation but the manifestation of Divine love to the world: "God so loved the world as to give His Only-begotten Son," and the Son Himself so loved men as to give Himself up for them. And to show that His love had attained the supreme degree, Christ Jesus willed that immediately after He had drawn His last breath on the Cross, His Heart should be pierced by the soldier's lance.

The love that is symbolised by the Heart in this devotion is first of all the created love of Jesus, but as He is the Incarnate Word, the treasures of this created love manifest to us the marvels of the Divine love of the Eternal Word.

THE PROPER and direct object of this devotion is therefore Christ's physical Heart. This Heart is indeed worthy of adoration because it forms part of His Human Nature and because the Word is united to a perfect nature. *Perfectus homo.* The same adoration that we give to the Divine Person of the Word reaches all that is personally united thereto. The Heart of Jesus is the Heart of God.

But the Heart which we honour, which we adore in this Humanity united to the Person of the Word, serves here as a symbol of love. When God says to us in the Scriptures: "My son, give Me thy heart," we understand that the heart here signifies love. We may say of someone: "I esteem him, I respect him, but I cannot give him my heart." We mean by these words that friendship, intimacy, and union are impossible.

In the devotion to the Sacred Heart of Jesus, we then honour the love that the Incarnate Word bears towards us.

Created love first of all. Christ Jesus is both God and Man, perfect God, perfect Man. This is the very mystery of the Incarnation. As "Son of Man," Christ has a heart like ours, a Heart of flesh, a Heart that beats for us with the tenderest, truest, noblest, and most faithful love that ever was. We have but to open the Gospel and on each page we shall see shine out the goodness, mercy, and condescension of Jesus towards mankind. We have seen how deeply human and infinitely delicate is this love.

This love of Christ is very real for it is founded upon the reality of the Incarnation itself. The Blessed Virgin, St. John, Magdalen, Lazarus, knew this well. It was not only a love of the will, but also a heartfelt love. When Christ Jesus said: "I have compassion on the multitude," He really felt the fibres of His human Heart moved by pity. When He saw Martha and Mary weeping for the toss of their brother, He wept with them; truly human tears were wrung from His Heart. Therefore the Jews who witnessed this sight said to one another: "Behold how He loved him."

Christ Jesus does not change. His Heart remains the most loving and most lovable that could ever be found.

WHENCE came this human love of Jesus, this created love? From the Uncreated and Divine love, from the love of the Eternal Word to which the Human Nature is indissolubly united. Although in Christ there are two perfect and distinct natures, keeping their specific energies and proper operations, there is only one Divine Person. The created love of Jesus is but the revelation of His uncreated love. Christ's Heart draws its human kindness from the ocean of the Divinity.

Upon Calvary we see Him die a Man like ourselves, One Who has been a prey to anguish, Who has been crushed beneath the weight of torments; we understand the love that this Man shows us. But this love is the concrete and tangible expression of the Divine love. The Heart of Jesus pierced upon the Cross reveals to us Christ's human love, but beneath the veil of the Humanity of Jesus is shown the ineffable and incomprehensible love of the Word.

LOVE alone can respond to love. Of what does Our Saviour complain to St. Margaret Mary? Of the lack of love in return for His love. "Behold this Heart that has so loved men and receives from them only ingratitude."

"Who will not love in return the One Who loves him? Who, being redeemed, will not love His Redeemer?"

> *Quis non amantem redamet?*
> *Quis non redemptus diligat?*
> (Hymn of Lauds for the Feast
> of the Sacred Heart)

This love to be perfect must bear a double character.

THERE is affective love consisting in the different feelings that move the heart towards a beloved person: admiration, complacency, joy, thanksgiving. This love gives birth to praise. Let us not fear to multiply our praises of the Heart of Jesus. The Litany of the Sacred Heart, acts of reparation and consecration, are so many expressions of this affective love, without which the human soul does not reach the perfection of its nature.

OF itself alone, however, this affective love is insufficient. To have all its value it must be manifested by deeds. "If you love Me," says Jesus Himself, "keep My commandments." That is the one touchstone. If we truly love Christ Jesus, not only shall we rejoice in His glory, not only shall we be saddened by the injuries done to His Heart, and offer Him honourable amends, but, above all, we shall strive to obey Him in all things, we shall accept readily all that His Providence ordains for us, we shall work to extend His reign in souls.

WHEN we receive Our Lord in Holy Communion, we possess within us that Divine Heart which is a furnace of love. Let us earnestly entreat that He will Himself grant us to understand this love, for one ray from on high is more effectual than all the light of human reasoning. Let us also entreat Him to enkindle within us a personal love for Him. "If by Our Lord's grace," says St. Teresa, "His love is imprinted one day in our hearts, all will become easy to us."

If this love for the Person of Jesus is in our heart, our activity will spring from it. We may meet with difficulties, undergo great trials and violent temptations; but if we love Christ Jesus, these difficulties, trials, and temptations will find us steadfast: *Aquæ multæ non potuerunt exstinguere caritatem.* For when the love of Christ urges us, we shall no longer wish to live for ourselves, but for Him Who loved us and delivered Himself up for us.

XVI

Christic the Crown
of All the Saints

CHRIST and the Church are inseparable; one is not to be conceived of without the other. This is why at the end of these conferences upon the Person of Jesus Christ and His mysteries we must speak of this Church which St. Paul calls the "completing" of Christ, and without which the mystery of Christ does not attain its perfection.

Here below this ineffable union is wrought by faith, grace, and charity; it is consummated in the splendours of Heaven and the Beatific Vision. Thus, having reached the end of the Liturgical Cycle, the Church celebrates in one solemn feast—the Feast of All Saints—the glory of the Kingdom of Jesus. It reunites in the same praise the entire company of the elect, for this company is one as Christ is one. To time succeeds eternity. Here below souls are formed to perfection, but the term is only to be found in this glorious company; moreover, our degree of beatitude is measured by the degree of charity attained at the hour when we leave this earth.

The first reason that we have for tending to holiness is "the will of God": *Hæc est voluntas Dei, sanctificatio vestra.*

God not only wills that we should be saved, but that we should become saints. God wills this because He Himself is holy. God is holiness itself; we are His creatures and He wishes the creature to reflect His image. Furthermore, He wills that, being His children, we should be perfect as He, our Heavenly Father, is perfect.

God finds His glory in our holiness. Each degree of holiness to which we attain, each sacrifice we make in order to acquire it, each virtue which is to adorn our souls will be a glory for God eternally.

So it is with the Saints. They stand "before the throne of God" and unceasingly render Him glory. The burning zeal of the Apostles, the testimony of the Martyrs, the profound knowledge of the Doctors, the dazzling purity of Virgins constitute so much homage to God.

It is, then, a lawful ambition for us to tend with all our might to gain for God this glory which He derives from our holiness. We ought fervently to aspire to a fellowship with that blessed company in which God Himself takes His delight.

In Heaven our holiness will be to contemplate the infinite light, to find in its splendour the source of all life and joy.

This light has come down into our valleys, tempering the infinite splendour of its beams beneath the veil of the Sacred Humanity. Christ Jesus, the Eternal Word, teaches us to look upon God, He reveals Himself to us. He says to us, "he that followeth Me, walketh not in darkness, but shall have the light of life."

What have we to do so as to walk in the light?

To be guided by the words of Jesus, by the maxims of His Gospel. Jesus tells us, for instance, that the blessed who possess His Kingdom are the poor in spirit, the meek, those who mourn, those who hunger and thirst after justice, the merciful, the clean of heart, the peacemakers, those who suffer persecution for justice' sake. We must believe Him, unite ourselves to Him by an act of faith, and lay the assent of our intellect down in homage at His feet. We must strive to live in humility, gentleness, mercy, purity, to keep peace with all, to bear contradiction.

NONE can say: holiness is not for me. God wills us to be saints for His glory and our joy. God does not mock us. When Our Lord says to us, "Be perfect," He knows all that He is asking of us, and He requires nothing above our power when we rely upon His grace.

He who would attempt to reach perfection by his own strength, would commit the sin of Lucifer who said: "I will exalt my throne above the stars of God. . . . I will ascend above the height of the clouds, I will be like the Most High." Satan was overthrown and cast down into the abyss.

As for us, what shall we say? What shall we do? We nourish the same ambition as this proud angel; we wish to reach the same height contemplated by him. But whilst he claimed to attain it of himself, we declare that without Christ Jesus we can do nothing. We say that it is with Christ and through Him that we can enter into the heavens.

THE DIFFERENCE that exists between the Saints and us does not arise from the greater number of difficulties that we have to overcome, but from the intensity of their faith in the word of Jesus Christ, and in the power of His grace, as besides from their greater generosity. We can, if we will, experience this for ourselves. Christ ever remains the same, as powerful, as magnificent in the distribution of His grace. The obstacles to the out-pourings of His gifts only lie in ourselves.

To honour the Saints is to declare that they are the realization of a divine idea, masterpieces of the grace of Jesus. God places His delight in them because they are the already glorious members of His beloved Son. They already make part of that resplendent kingdom won by Jesus for the glory of His Father.

Moreover we ought to invoke them. Doubtless Christ Jesus is our one Mediator. We have access to the Father only through Him. Christ, however—not to diminish His mediation, but to extend it—wills that the princes of the Heavenly Court should offer Him our prayers which He Himself presents to His Father.

To these relations of homage and prayer that unite us to the Saints we ought to add our efforts to resemble the Saints. We should have a firm and sincere longing for perfection, an effectual will to respond fully to the merciful designs of our divine predestination in Jesus.

Our miseries are very real; our weaknesses, our limitations we know well enough, but God knows them better than we do. And the sense of our frailty—recognized and avowed—honours God. There is in God one perfection wherein He wills to be eternally glorified, a perfection which is perhaps the key of all that befalls us here below: it is mercy. Mercy is love in the face of misery; if there were no misery there would be no mercy. The Angels declare God's holiness; but, as for us, we shall be in heaven the living witnesses to the divine mercy; in crowning our works, God crowns the gift of His mercy.

Let us no longer be discouraged by trials and disappointments. They will be so much the greater and deeper in proportion as God calls us higher. God has a powerful hand, and His purifying operations reach depths that only the saints know. By the temptations that He permits, by the adversities that He sends, by the desolations and terrible loneliness in which He sometimes leaves the soul, He tries it so as to detach it from all that is created. He digs deep down into it in order to empty it of self.

God places His mercy in beatifying us. All the sufferings He permits or sends are so many titles to heavenly bliss.

In Heaven we shall understand that all God's mercies had their point of departure on Calvary, and that the Blood of Jesus is the price of the heavenly gladness which we shall then for evermore enjoy. The river of beatitude which eternally flows in this City of God has its source in the sacrifice of our Divine High Priest.

If during our life we have followed Jesus; if each year

we have contemplated Him with faith and love in the cycle of His mysteries, while striving to imitate Him and abide in union with Him, we may be assured that the constant prayer which He offers for us to His Father will be answered. By His Spirit, He will imprint His living image upon our souls; the Father will recognize us at the last day as members of His Son and will make us co-heirs with Him.

www.ingramcontent.com/pod-product-compliance
Lightning Source LLC
Chambersburg PA
CBHW030501100426
42813CB00002B/306